I0479246

PIVOT FOR

PLANET:

BUSINESS

LESSONS FROM A

MODERN

PANDEMIC

Mustafa Ozer

Copyright © 2023 Mustafa Ozer

All rights reserved.

ISBN: 9798378171897

Cover Illustration: Hsin Hsu

DEDICATION

To all those who faced the trials of the modern pandemic with strength and adaptability.

To the innovative minds and caring souls who strived not only for business success but also for the well-being of our planet.

This book is dedicated to the visionaries who embraced change, learned valuable lessons, and turned challenges into chances.

May your actions inspire generations to come, showing us that with determination and courage, we can steer towards a brighter, more compassionate world.

CONTENTS

The space between heaven and earth is like a bellows.

The shape changes but not the form.

The more it moves, the more it yields.

More words count less; hold fast to the center.

道德經 Dao De Jing by Lao Tsu translated by Gi-fu Feng and
Jane English with Toinette Lippe Publisher Everyman's Library

.

CHAPTER 1: HOW TO MANAGE DAY ZERO?

The pandemic has triggered a series of major changes, not just for individuals but for businesses too. Many businesses lost, and those that did survive have been altered forever. Good leaders and effective founders are using such pivotal moments to create new ways of working and doing business instead of waiting for things to go back to the way they were. Instead of failing to adapt, the most successful leaders have used the crisis to their advantage, seeing it as an opportunity to find new and innovative ways of operating. They understood that managing the initial days of a crisis correctly could set the stage for long-term success.

By embracing change and reframing challenges as opportunities, these leaders demonstrated a willingness to break free from the confines of the past and forge new paths forward. The lessons learned from their experiences provide valuable insights that can guide us in navigating the complexities of crises and finding clarity amidst uncertainty as well as success in otherwise hard times. Managing the initial days of a crisis correctly, similar to the ways that surviving businesses did with COVID-19, can be made easier with positive inertia. We'll dive more into this later. For now, it is a challenge to sense make what is stirring. So, to do so, let's first reflect back on the pandemic.

When the director of WHO announced in March 2020 that the novel coronavirus was a pandemic based on the 13-fold number of cases, the world was caught unprepared, and it would be wrong to assume that it was something we were not expecting. In fact, it was long overdue. But before diving into the crisis, let's travel back to a time before the pandemic, to a darkly lit room where thought leaders, business owners, and politicians were debating documents full of complicated graphs. These graphs show that the signal and data indicate that the world is in fact ready for a pandemic to come. This event was a quick exercise hosted at the Johns Hopkins Center for Health Security in partnership with the World Economic Forum and the Bill and Melinda Gates Foundation. The name of the session was Event 201, a high-level pandemic exercise on October 18, 2019, in New York, NY. The exercise illustrated areas where public/private partnerships will be necessary during the response to a severe pandemic in order to diminish large-scale economic and societal consequences. When this event was being held, the nurturing ground for a perfect storm to come was gathering clouds on the horizon, just a few short months before WHO declared the pandemic and the plunge of the world economy. So, even though leaders globally were expecting such a crisis, many were clearly unprepared.

The key question here is: *Is it possible to prepare ourselves for unexpected adversaries, and how can we manage the initial stage of such crises?* The answer lies in mental models. Mental models can help us navigate the complexities and uncertainties that are bound to arise. Mental models provide frameworks for understanding and responding to unprecedented challenges, allowing us to identify patterns, anticipate consequences, and make informed decisions.

As we reflect back on the pandemic, it becomes evident that while the world may have been caught off guard, the signs were there for those who were willing to pay attention. Event 201 serves as a stark reminder that foresight and preparedness are crucial in mitigating the impact of unforeseen adversities. It highlights the importance of proactive measures, collaborative efforts, and the need for resilient systems that can withstand and respond to such challenges.

During times of crisis, mental models can serve as guiding principles, enabling leaders to quickly assess the situation, gather relevant information, and devise effective strategies. They help us make sense of what is stirring by providing a lens through which we can interpret events and discern the underlying dynamics at play. By embracing a growth mindset and a willingness to adapt, leaders can leverage these mental models to navigate uncharted territory and seize opportunities for growth and transformation. Here is how:

Navigating a Crisis: The Three Mental Models All Businesses Should Know

Amidst the challenges posed by black swan events like the pandemic, it becomes imperative for businesses to equip themselves with mental models that can guide their response and recovery. The three mental models that are particularly relevant in navigating a crisis are resilience, agility, and adaptive leadership. As we reflect on the lessons learned from the pandemic, it is essential to recognize the value of these mental models in preparing for the looming meta crisis induced by climate change and other unpredictable challenges that lie ahead. However, before we dive into these mental models and how businesses and leaders can use them, we must first understand what causes them to be needed in the first place... the black swan event.

In the world of investment and finance, the black swan event is the one type of event that no one ever wants to happen. A black swan event refers to an unpredictable, unforeseen, and unforeseeable event that causes massive social and economic impact, such as an economic crash or market correction. Black swan events are typically rare, so the economic damage that they cause can be enormous and long-lasting. While it was not an unexpected event itself, the pandemic and our response to it can provide meaningful lessons for future events. In fact, we must dive deeper into the lessons learned from the pandemic in order to avoid similar consequences from such an event in the future as we are entering an age of meta crisis induced by climate change.

One of the earliest lessons we learned from the COVID-19 crisis was the importance of detecting these events before they happen in order to avoid economic devastation. As a long proponent of course correction, introspection & retrospection, I often meditate over Soren Kierkegaard's wise words on how life can be only understood by looking back while it must be lived forward. Following his footsteps, it is important to look for insights. This work is heavily inspired by Slowdown Papers[1], which was an early sensemaking series written by Dan Hill. Drawing inspiration from this, we are reminded of the value of taking a deliberate and thoughtful approach to understanding complex situations. The Slowdown Papers provided a platform for deep reflection and analysis, encouraging us to slow down and critically examine the underlying dynamics and implications of the crisis. This deliberate pace allows us to uncover insights that may otherwise go unnoticed in the rush of everyday life. In the context of crisis response, this introspective approach becomes paramount. It prompts us to question

---

[1] Slowdown Papers by Dan Hill: https://medium.com/slowdown-papers

assumptions, challenge conventional wisdom, and explore alternative perspectives.

By engaging in a process of deep sensemaking, we can better understand the root causes and interconnectedness of the crisis, as well as identify the emerging patterns and weak signals that may be harbingers of future challenges.

Furthermore, this introspective mindset encourages course correction, enabling us to adjust our strategies and actions in light of new information and changing circumstances. It embraces the idea that flexibility and adaptability are crucial in navigating uncharted territory. Rather than clinging to rigid plans and preconceived notions, we remain open to new insights and willing to make necessary adjustments along the way. In fact, this is a crucial aspect of maintaining a successful business in an ever-changing landscape.

Now, before we dive even deeper into navigating such crises, let's do a quick flashback to the early days of COVID to focus on how to spot a black swan event. Once we go over how to spot such an event, we can go into how we can avoid the long-lasting consequences.

Similar to the pandemic, a black swan event is an unpredictable and highly impactful event. They are rare, but when they happen, they can have a major effect on a company, organization, or even a country. For instance, when Uber launched their self-driving cars in Pittsburgh in 2016, it was heralded as one of their best ideas to date. But shortly after the launch, their self-driving car killed a pedestrian crossing the street. This was a huge problem for Uber and had a direct impact on how people viewed their new technology. It's important to know what you're getting into before investing time and money into an idea that may not have been thought out well enough. This unpredictable and highly impactful event is merely a minor example of the consequences that unpreparedness can bring. For events like the pandemic, we need sandbox environments to stress test such events. Nassim Taleb lists other black swan events including the rise of the Internet, the personal computer, World War I, the dissolution of the Soviet Union, and September 11, 2001.

The likelihood of a pandemic was always calculated, it was known to experts and politicians, yet inertia was there to stay. The numbers on graphs or simulation exercises are just numbers, but inertia in masses and policies are both realities of modern times. So, even when the risk is identified, it takes a huge effort to break the inertia.

The relevance of the law of inertia becomes apparent when we apply it to both individuals and organizations. In physics, the law of inertia elucidates that an object will persist in its current state, be it at rest or in motion, unless acted upon by an external force. Similarly, humans and organizations often exhibit a tendency to maintain the status quo until compelled by external circumstances to initiate change. While the inevitability of a pandemic was widely acknowledged, it was not until the actual crisis unfolded that we were motivated to take action and implement necessary transformations. This inertia is not unique to individuals alone; it also manifests in the decisions made by founders and their businesses. Just as an object at rest requires a force to set it in motion, founders often need the impetus of external factors to prompt them to pivot their business models or adapt their product offerings. However, many founders didn't realize how much they'd truly have to adjust their businesses when COVID-19 hit.

Taleb argues that our inability to forecast unexpected and rare events like black swans leads us to undervalue their significance and overestimate our understanding of the world, resulting in making bad decisions and being excessively confident in our predictions and plans. This can be considered a cognitive bias, which is a pattern of thinking or decision-making that strays from rationality or objectivity in interpreting information. Although Taleb does not categorize COVID as a black swan event since it was predicted to happen this century, I believe that there is a potential black swan element in our response to the pandemic, especially given the long-lasting consequences on the entire world. Our cognitive biases may have led us to underestimate the severity of a pandemic, assuming it would be limited to the scale of previous epidemics like MERS.

Looking back to previous coronavirus outbreaks before, we had the SARS outbreak in 2003[2] and the MERS outbreak in 2012 both of which were stopped by a combination of infection control methods[3] and luck[4]. However, with a behemoth like China, the gravity of inertia was enormous, hence the reaction time was long. Considering the early days of the pandemic, it all started with a few deaths in Wuhan, China, with the earliest reported case on November 17, 2019. By December 31, 2019, when the Chinese authorities first reported it to the World Health Organization (WHO), it was already a full-fledged outbreak and within just 3 more months it was

---

[2] CDC Factsheet on SARS
[3] https://theconversation.com/the-original-sars-virus-disappeared-heres-why-coronavirus-wont-do-the-same-138177

classified as a pandemic.

So, what were the cognitive biases that created an inertia in our collective response? During my research with entrepreneurs who worked to find a response in the early days of lockdowns, I've asked what the underlying biases are that blinded us. Based on their answers, there are 3 cognitive biases that kicked in: normality bias, overconfidence bias, and Semmelweis Reflex.

Let's look at them in detail.

- Normality bias: This bias causes people to believe that things will always continue as they have in the past, and that extreme events are unlikely to occur. In the context of the pandemic, people may have assumed that previous disease outbreaks had been contained quickly, like the SARS and MERS outbreaks, and that the same would be true for COVID-19. This led to a delayed response and a failure to adequately prepare.

Japan, South Korea, and the United States confirmed their first case of COVID-19 approximately three weeks after the reported outbreak in China. From then on, disease progression within these countries varied quite a bit. While it took 42 days to reach 100 confirmed cases in the U.S., Japan reached that number in 31 days and South Korea in 29 days. However, instances like social distancing, the move to remote work, and other initiatives or measures were instituted much later.

- Overconfidence bias: This bias leads people to believe that they are more knowledgeable or skilled than they are, leading to overestimation of their ability to handle complex or uncertain situations. This could manifest in a false sense of security or optimism about the pandemic's impact, leading to inadequate preparations or a lack of precautionary measures.

An example of overconfidence bias related to COVID-19 can be seen in the initial response by some governments, organizations, and individuals. Many believed that the virus would not spread as widely as it did, and that it would not have as serious an impact as it ultimately did. As a result, some governments and organizations did not take adequate precautionary measures, such as stockpiling medical supplies or implementing lockdowns, to prepare for the worst-case scenario. During emergency situations, just-in-time logistics are not effective, as there is not enough time to properly plan and execute these logistics. A rapid lesson that can be learned from this is the need for alternative logistics (mostly local) methods during such situations.

- Semmelweis Reflex: This refers to the tendency of people to reject new information or evidence that contradicts their beliefs or established norms. In the context of the pandemic, this could manifest as resistance to implementing new measures, such as wearing masks or social distancing, due to a reluctance to deviate from established norms or beliefs about personal freedoms.

The Semmelweis Reflex refers to the resistance to new information or evidence that contradicts established norms or beliefs. This resistance can lead to a delayed or inadequate response to unexpected events, such as the COVID-19 pandemic.

In contrast, Bridges' theory of change[5] emphasizes the importance of acknowledging and embracing the uncertainty and ambiguity that come with change. According to the theory, the process of change involves three stages: endings, transitions, and new beginnings. By embracing these stages, individuals and communities can more effectively adapt to change and move towards a new beginning.

In the context of COVID-19, the Semmelweis Reflex may have led to resistance to adopting new measures, such as wearing masks or practicing social distancing. However, by embracing Bridges' theory of change, individuals and communities can acknowledge the uncertainty and ambiguity surrounding the pandemic and move towards new beginnings.

For example, instead of resisting new measures due to preexisting beliefs or norms, individuals and communities can acknowledge the need for change and embrace the uncertainty that comes with it. This

---

[5] Developed by William Bridges, Bridges' Theory of Change emphasizes managing emotional aspects of change over time. It involves three stages: Ending (letting go), Neutral Zone (uncertainty), and New Beginning (embracing change).

can involve accepting that the pandemic is a new reality that requires new ways of thinking and acting and embracing the changes needed to adapt to this reality. By embracing the need for change and acknowledging the uncertainty and ambiguity that come with it, individuals and communities can move beyond the Semmelweis Reflex and more effectively adapt to unexpected events like the COVID-19 pandemic.

These biases may have contributed to a lack of preparedness and slow response in the early days of the pandemic. It is important to recognize these biases and actively work to overcome them to make better decisions in the face of unexpected events.

The WEF Global Risk Landscape 2020 report shows that while the likelihood of a pandemic was low, the impact was beyond the threshold to make it a considerable threat.

One of the early learnings from COVID-19 was that black swan events can happen at any time. No matter how prepared you are, you cannot stop their catastrophic potential from happening. The second-best thing can be softening the impact, which was famously coined as "flattening the curve" in the early days of the pandemic. Indeed, COVID-19 was a novel event but it was far from being an unexpected event that we weren't ready for. If we had been more prepared to deal with the pandemic, we would've had other, more productive measures in place before having to flatten the curve. We could have had this level of preparedness if we had known the telltale signs of a black swan event.

Decoding the Cryptic Clues: Unveiling the Telltale Signs of an Impending Black Swan Event

While black swan events may seem sudden and unexpected, they are often preceded by cryptic clues that can offer glimpses into the brewing storm. Just as a tree's changing leaves or the sea's production of mucilage indicate disruptions in their respective ecosystems, there are indicators in human systems that can hint at the emergence of an anomaly. By paying attention to these telltale signs and honing our ability to interpret them, we can enhance our preparedness and response, potentially softening the impact of future black swan events.

To get an idea of how we can use the identification of these telltale signs to avoid long-lasting consequences, let's look at some previous black swan events and how we might have been able to prevent them or minimize their impact.

- Global Financial Crisis: The Global Financial Crisis of 2008 resulted from a complex combination of factors, including lax lending standards, the proliferation of complex financial instruments, and the housing market bubble. If regulators had recognized the warning signs and taken steps to rein in risky lending practices and regulate the financial industry more closely, the crisis might have been averted or minimized.

- Fukushima Nuclear Disaster: The Fukushima nuclear disaster in 2011 was caused by a massive earthquake and tsunami that damaged the Fukushima Daiichi nuclear power plant in Japan. If the plant's operators had taken better precautions and had more effective emergency response plans in place, they might have been able to prevent or mitigate the damage caused by the disaster.

- Deepwater Horizon Oil Spill: The Deepwater Horizon oil spill in 2010 was caused by an explosion on an oil rig in the Gulf of Mexico. If BP and other oil companies had taken more precautions and had better safety protocols in place, they might have been able to prevent the explosion and the subsequent oil spill that caused significant environmental and economic damage.

That being said, telltale signs or temperature checks require constant energy for being ready to react, which is not how our species are biologically evolved. Our mind is excellent at preserving energy and looking only at relevant signs that are obvious and right in front of us. So, it is smart to train our brains to detect several telltale signs to predict crises.

Here are some telltale signs of economic and environmental problems that are highly indicative of a pending crisis:

- *VIX* index: The *VIX* index, also known as the "Fear Index," is a measure of market volatility and is often used as an indicator of economic instability. A high *VIX* index indicates that investors are uncertain about the future and may be preparing for a downturn.

- Drewry Shipping Index: The Drewry Shipping Index is a measure of the cost of shipping goods and commodities around the world. A sudden increase in the cost of shipping can be an indication of environmental problems, such as natural disasters, that disrupt global supply chains.

- Sentiment Analysis: With the rise of artificial intelligence and machine learning, sentiment analysis can be a powerful tool for spotting an impending crisis. By monitoring social media, news outlets, customer feedback, employee feedback, and the stock market, sentiment analysis can identify early warning signs of a crisis and help businesses and organizations take proactive steps to mitigate its impact.

Identifying early signs of potential problems is crucial for ensuring timely and effective interventions. It is possible to list early signs for each and every situation, and this is why it is important to assess the current landscape and pick relevant indicators for an organization, city, country, region, and the planet. By doing so, we can stay ahead of potential crises and take proactive measures to mitigate their impact. With a collective effort to identify and address early warning signs, we can work towards a safer and more resilient future.

As a startup, it's important to be aware of potential red flags that could hinder your success. That way, you can avoid situations like Uber, which failed to prepare for how their self-driving cars could turn out. Here are some early warning indicators for founders to keep in mind:

Lack of a clear market opportunity: Without a clear understanding of your target market and their needs, it's difficult to build a successful business. Keep a close eye on market trends and customer feedback to ensure that you're staying relevant.

Insufficient capital: Running out of money is a common reason why startups fail. Keep a close eye on your cash flow and consider raising additional capital if necessary.

High turnover: Losing talent and key employees can be a major setback for any startup. Make sure you're offering competitive salaries and benefits, and prioritize creating a positive work culture.

Unclear governance: As your startup grows, it's important to establish clear roles and responsibilities for each team member. This will help avoid confusion and ensure everyone is working towards the same goals.

Poor work-life balance: Burnout is a real risk for startup founders and employees. Make sure you're encouraging work-life balance and providing opportunities for rest and relaxation.

By monitoring these early warning signs and taking action when necessary, you can help ensure the long-term success of your startup.

Finding the Signal Through the Noise: Data, Divination and Social Listening

As the world scrambled to find a solution, vaccine developments were finalized with unprecedented speed. However, a new challenge emerged: getting more people to accept the vaccine. The World Health Organization (WHO) faced a daunting task as anti-vaccine campaigns spread misinformation about the vaccine's safety and efficacy.

WHO knew that a successful vaccination campaign would require mobilizing young people to be a leverage for information campaigns. However, this turned out to be a big challenge, as young people were a key target for the anti-vaccine movement. In response, WHO Europe collaborated with a few social innovators, including me, to find the signal through the noise and collect insights on how to approach the youth and mobilize them for vaccination campaigns.

Through the workshops, including stakeholder mapping and social listening, we found that young people were concerned about the vaccine's safety and efficacy. There was a need for a campaign that would address these concerns head-on. While stakeholder mapping is a term related to impact modeling, we have heavily used it to understand how global ambitions find a reflection in local communities. Using social listening, we also discovered that young people were more likely to trust information from their peers rather than from authorities or traditional media outlets.

With these insights, the WHO team developed a campaign that focused on peer-to-peer messaging and leveraged social media platforms like Instagram and TikTok to communicate with young people. The campaign featured young people sharing their experiences of getting vaccinated and dispelling myths about the vaccine.

The campaign's success in mobilizing young people for vaccination was impressive. Many young people shared their vaccination experiences on social media and encouraged their peers to do the same. The campaign received significant media coverage, with news outlets highlighting the innovative approach and its success in engaging young people.

The collaboration between WHO Europe and the Global Shapers community is an excellent example of how finding signal through noise is crucial in tackling complex challenges. The team discovered valuable insights by engaging with young people and involving them in the campaign's development. By finding the right approach that resonated with young people, the campaign was able to cut through the noise of misinformation and successfully mobilize young people for vaccination.

In the meantime, the World Health Organization developed a platform called Early AI-supported Response with Social Listening (EARS) to gather, analyze, and share data from online conversations related to the COVID-19 pandemic. The platform collects data from open digital and social media content and uses automated approaches to identify emerging narratives at the country level. Although currently focused on the COVID-19 virus and vaccine content, EARS can be adapted to search for other topics in the future, such as routine immunization. The platform can incorporate structured and unstructured data, and offline content can also be included if reports are entered into a digital format.

The Map is Not the Territory

Amidst the complexities of predicting and preparing for rare and unpredictable events, such as a pandemic, it becomes crucial to acknowledge the limitations of our models and embrace alternative approaches. Alfred Korzybski's notion that "the map is not the territory" serves as a reminder that our representations of reality are imperfect and require interpretation.

Alfred Korzybski, a philosopher and engineer of Polish-American origin, coined the phrase "the map is not the territory". Its purpose was to illustrate how people tend to mistake representations of reality for reality itself. Korzybski believed that models are intended to serve as representations of objects, but they are not identical to those objects. Even the best models require interpretation, and they are inherently imperfect since they are simplified abstractions of a more complex reality. Additionally, we tend to underestimate their limitations and prefer a flawed model over having no model at all, which is a natural human tendency.

Given the number of telltale indicators and a plethora of weak but significant signals, some experts claim that it is impossible to predict not only the occurrence but also the timing of such a rare and unpredictable event. However, this research gives us a sneak peek at how Neural Networks and machine learning can act as early warning systems. In this search by IJCAI[6], Diversely Extrapolated Neural Networks that fit the training data and are able to generalize more diversely when extrapolating to novel data points. Their conclusion is having the ability to train diverse functions to have uncertain predictions is promising. While this sounds highly complex and scientific, this is a modern version of divination. If you don't have access to quantum computers and datasets to feed super-intelligent AI, according to Bernard Shaw, throwing coins can be your second-best option.

Given the unpredictable nature of black swan events, some experts believe it's impossible to predict both their occurrence and timing. However, recent research has provided insights into how Neural Networks and machine learning can act as early warning systems for such events. Diversely Extrapolated Neural Networks have shown promising results, but this might seem complex and scientific to some. DENNs, although complex in their underlying technology, can be understood through their

---

[6] Proceedings of the Twenty-Ninth International Joint Conference on Artificial Intelligence, pages 2140-2147

fundamental principle of training diverse functions with uncertain predictions. By leveraging large datasets and sophisticated algorithms, DENNs can analyze patterns, identify weak signals, and extrapolate trends to make informed predictions about the occurrence and timing of black swan events. This technology harnesses the power of computational modeling and pattern recognition to provide insights that were previously inaccessible. While the scientific nature of DENNs may seem intimidating, it is essential to recognize the potential they hold for enhancing early warning systems.

When a crisis like COVID-19 hits, decision-makers must navigate a complex and rapidly evolving landscape, which is why such effective early warning systems are so crucial. In these situations, the concept of "the map is not the territory" becomes crucial to understand as our mental models and perceptions may not always match the complexity of the real-world situation. Who else remembers how we collectively underestimated the duration of the pandemic during the early days? No one knew how long it would take, but it was never going to be quick. "It could be anywhere from four to six weeks to up to three months," Former Chief Medical Advisor to the President of the United States once said, ''No one knows how long that will take, but it won't be quick. It could be anywhere from four to six weeks to up to three months." Even after almost half a decade, we are still facing the virus, albeit with a lesser impact but no one knows when it will completely vanish or turn into a seasonal flu. In the face of such uncertainty and complexity, the concept of "map is not territory" becomes crucial to understand. This concept suggests that our mental models and maps of reality may not always match the complexity of the real-world situation. In other words, we need to be aware that our perceptions may not be accurate or complete.

In this section, we will explore how the concept of "map is not territory" played out in the experiences of several founders who responded to the COVID-19 crisis in different ways. As the new managing director of a social innovation platform and social incubation, imece, I was faced with the challenge of growing the organization's profitability. However, the existing business model of offering a startup-only accelerator program was costly and not scaling well. It was not until the pandemic hit that I realized our strategic plans were obsolete, like old maps. Being a new manager during the early days of the pandemic was challenging. The previous paths designed for a pre-pandemic were almost obsolete and needed to be pivoted in order to thrive in the organization that I was trusted to manage.

COVID-19 presented a new reality and landscape that forced our team to reassess the situation and come up with a new way of doing things. By examining how I managed a team of five, we were able to pivot our value proposition from a startup-only accelerator operation to an open-innovation platform for complex problems. This shift in our narration helped us to triple our revenue while enabling our organization to open up its partnership structure by having its first paying clients during the pandemic.

This was only possible because, as a newly assigned managing director, I recognized that the pandemic had created a new reality, which meant that our previous mental model or *map* of how our organization operated was no longer accurate. By shifting our value proposition, we were able to adapt to the changing landscape and provide value to our clients in a new and innovative way. The lesson learned from this experience is that leaders and decision-makers must remain agile and adaptable in the face of a crisis. The concept of "map is not territory" highlights the importance of constantly re-evaluating our mental models and assumptions and being open to new ways of thinking and doing things.

We should also be proactive in preparing for potential black swan events. This is especially true given that we don't know when they will happen and can have a big impact on our society and economy. We recommend that you start by developing a plan to prepare for disasters. It doesn't matter if it is a natural disaster or not, your plan needs to include steps to protect your business from all types of disasters like power outages, hardware failures, and network outages. When developing this plan, ask yourself: What would happen if your organization lost its data center for 3 days due to an unforeseen event? What about 10 days? How about 30 days? Once you've considered these questions, list what must be done to recover from the loss of your data center.

It was still early in COVID-19 and we had a lot to learn. But as we learned more about the pandemic, one thing became clear: if we didn't detect these things, they not only could become unstoppable but have an immense impact on our systems and communities. How would we know they were coming? What would happen if they were too late? We knew that sometimes even when you're looking for them, you might not see them coming. This is the same for other pending or even imminent crises including the climate crisis, but this is something to be discussed later in this series. Let's focus on the pandemic and try to find out the learnings that we can apply to pivot our strategies.

CHAPTER 2: EMPIRE OF FEAR

The *name* that *can be named* is not the eternal *name*
Dao De Jing 1

When I was a fellow at the Capra Course delivered by
Fritjof Capra, I was immensely captivated by the notion of
connectedness with our nature. The fellowship was around
the earlier work of Capra and in his book titled "The
Systems View of Life," we were studying life as systems
comprised of interconnected networks. Even though many
people felt social distancing, when I look back at the
pandemic, I feel nostalgic about the sense of
connectedness we experienced in many different aspects
of our daily lives.

While there were many reasons to feel disconnected and
distant, I still remember the joy of people exploring their

passion by baking their own bread, the warmth of shared lockdown experiences, and the collective fear surrounding the unknown. Such emotions, including fear and love, have been the subject of long studies in different disciplines. Let's dive deeper into fear and how it made us all more connected than ever during COVID-19.

The COVID-19 pandemic was a significant source of fear for many people worldwide. While fear is a natural human response to perceived danger, it can also be overwhelming and have negative effects on mental health.

Aristotle's analysis of fear can offer insights into how we can approach and manage our fears related to COVID-19. Fear is a universal emotion that affects not only human beings but also animals. This suggests that fear is a natural response to a perceived threat, and we should not feel ashamed or weak for experiencing it. In fact, just knowing that it connected us all during COVID-19 can shed light on the fact that it *is* a natural emotion for all animals.

However, Aristotle also notes that fear can be influenced by our perception of the situation and our ability to evaluate the intentions of others. In the case of COVID-19, misinformation and conflicting information about the virus and its origins have heightened fears and anxiety for many individuals.

One important lesson we can learn from Aristotle's analysis of fear is the importance of critically evaluating information and sources to ensure that our fears are grounded in reality rather than irrational fears based on inaccurate information. By staying informed and taking necessary precautions, we can manage our fears and help prevent the spread of COVID-19. In this chapter, we will observe the role of fear in shaping our collective experience of the pandemic.

Owning Our Fears - The Power in Naming Them

Ever since the COVID-19 pandemic, fear has become a prevalent emotion for many people worldwide. We are afraid of contracting the virus, spreading it to others, and experiencing its long-term effects on our lives. Naming our feelings of fear can be a powerful tool for managing them. By identifying and labeling our emotions, we can begin to understand and process them and look at them objectively, rather than letting them consume us.

Moreover, naming our fears can help us feel more in control. When we are afraid, we often feel powerless and vulnerable. However, by giving our fear a name, we can begin to take ownership of it and find ways to manage it. For example, if we fear catching the virus, we can name that fear: *I have the fear of contracting COVID-19.* From there, we can find ways to manage this fear. Now that we know exactly what we're afraid of, we can take steps to protect ourselves, such as wearing a mask and practicing social distancing. This will, in turn, decrease our fear and help us cope with it in healthy ways. Naming the fear itself will also allow us to validate our emotions and become more self-aware about how we feel.

In times of uncertainty, naming our emotions can also help us feel more grounded. The COVID-19 pandemic has disrupted many aspects of our lives, and it can be challenging to make sense of it all. But naming our feelings of fear and anxiety can help. The name we need to embrace is polycrisis, a concept that of mutually reinforcing sets of threats to what we used to conceive of as "order".

In the polycrisis age, the moods and emotions felt today have an impact on people's choices and decisions regarding risk. These emotions, like fear, are what shape our collective experience of such events. One tool to measure collective fear and its impact on the economy is a tool called The Fear and Greed Index, which dropped to extreme fear levels in March 2020. Who else remembers the scene that went viral on TV and social media? The scene involved several instances of people in hazmat suits attending to unconscious individuals, one of whom was alone in a corridor. There was also a wide roadblock manned by people in white lab coats, masks, and vests. These clips instilled fear in people worldwide, heightening our joined fear.

In the face of this unprecedented health crisis, many of us have felt fear in ways we never have before. Unlike the Spanish Flu, which occurred at the end of the First World War, COVID-19 has dominated the news cycle. Moreover, the global sentiment and the economic and geopolitical consequences of the Spanish flu were ultimately rather minor.

That being said, no pandemic in recent history has caused permanent changes to society or an irreversible erosion of civil liberties. Frank Furedi, the author of "How Fear Works" points out that during the Spanish Flu, the American President Wilson made no remarks on the pandemic, and there were no lockdowns.

However, fear was the dominant feeling during the COVID-19 pandemic. Unlike previous pandemics, the COVID-19 pandemic unfolded in an era where global communication and information sharing are more accessible than ever before. News of the virus spread quickly through various media channels and social platforms, often leading to the amplification of fear-inducing messages and the rapid dissemination of misinformation. The pervasive fear had profound consequences on individuals and communities, shaping their behaviors, attitudes, and decision-making processes.

Governments and health authorities responded to the prevailing fear by implementing a range of measures aimed at mitigating the spread of the virus. These measures included widespread lockdowns, travel restrictions, social distancing guidelines, and the enforcement of mask mandates. While these actions were undertaken with the intention of safeguarding public health, they also fueled the existing fear and contributed to a climate of uncertainty and anxiety.

The impact of fear during the pandemic extended beyond the immediate health concerns. It influenced various aspects of society, including the economy, education, and mental well-being. Businesses faced unprecedented challenges, with many forced to shut down or adapt to remote operations. Schools and educational institutions had to swiftly transition to online learning platforms, disrupting traditional classroom settings. Moreover, individuals experienced heightened levels of stress, anxiety, and social isolation, as fear shaped their interactions and daily routines.

Although fear played a significant role in shaping the narrative of the pandemic, it is essential to recognize that fear is a complex and multifaceted emotion. While it can motivate individuals to take necessary precautions and prioritize their safety, it can also lead to irrational decision-making, the spread of misinformation, and a sense of societal division.

As we start to emerge from the pandemic, it's important to reflect on what we've learned about fear. The COVID-19 pandemic has brought with it a host of emotions, including fear. Fear is a natural and instinctive response to danger and uncertainty, and it can be both helpful and harmful. In small doses, fear can motivate us to take action and stay safe. But when fear is constant and overwhelming, it can become paralyzing and have a negative impact on our mental health and well-being. It was the first feeling we experienced, and it was fear that was communicated in the early stages of the pandemic. Even after two years, due to the zero-COVID policy in China, fear still persisted.

Are you wondering why it's worth investing a significant amount of time in understanding and defining our fears? As entrepreneurs, we frequently encounter various fears, such as imposter syndrome, the unease of disappointing our customers or investors, the constant worry of meeting financial obligations like rent and salaries, and the fear of becoming overwhelmed by our work. However, by acknowledging and explicitly identifying these fears, we take the crucial first step toward conquering them. Moreover, developing the skill of collectively navigating fear is vital for fostering resilience and unity within our communities, encompassing our colleagues, consumers, beneficiaries, users, and investors.

In a similar fashion, Harvard Business Review approached around 600 CEOs and requested them to identify the most significant challenges that are causing them anxiety during the ongoing global COVID-19 pandemic. Indeed the pandemic has caused a significant influx of information and the need to adapt to new behaviors. Many CEOs and founders were facing unprecedented challenges in their personal and professional lives, resulting in a collective sense of grief. To navigate this crisis and position their companies for success in the future, HBR identified that leaders including founders must consider two key questions: How can we emerge stronger than competitors in our industry? and How can we learn from this experience to thrive in a new world?

Leaders are advised to embrace to two guiding principles: protecting the core and maintaining the business in the present while simultaneously planning for its transformation in the future. This can be achieved by focusing on two main approaches: *protecting the core* aspects of the business and seizing new opportunities by *pivoting for the planet.*

Protecting the core involves safeguarding the essential elements of the business that are crucial for its survival, such as maintaining financial stability, ensuring the well-being of employees, and preserving relationships with users, customers, and stakeholders. Pivoting, on the other hand, requires a proactive approach to identify and capitalize on emerging opportunities. This involves exploring what is emerging in the new markets, and reevaluating business models and purpose, with innovative strategies to adapt to the changing landscape.

By following these principles and considering the two P's (protect the core and pivot to new opportunities), organizations can navigate the current crisis while preparing themselves for future success. Whether it is the core protection or future pivoting, there is a need to name what is emerging together with our stakeholders.

The pandemic has demonstrated the power of collective action and the importance of coming together to protect one another. By understanding the role fear plays in shaping our responses, we can foster empathy and support for those experiencing heightened anxiety or distress. Compassion and solidarity can help alleviate fear and create a sense of togetherness, allowing us to face challenges as a united front.

Moreover, learning to navigate fear can empower us to make informed decisions based on reliable information on what to protect and where to pivot. Fear can make us more susceptible to misinformation and conspiracy theories, as uncertainty breeds vulnerability. By recognizing this tendency, we can cultivate critical thinking skills and engage in fact-checking and verifying information before accepting it as truth. This enables us to make well-informed choices that contribute to the well-being of ourselves and society as a whole.

Additionally, understanding fear and its impact can help us shape policies and responses that address the root causes of fear and mitigate its negative effects. By recognizing the societal and psychological implications of fear, policymakers and health authorities can design strategies that prioritize public well-being while minimizing unnecessary fear and anxiety. Creating transparent and trustworthy communication channels can also help build trust and counteract the spread of misinformation, enabling individuals to navigate fear more effectively.

Here are the three main lessons we can take with us as we move forward to collectively navigate fear more effectively:

Fear is a Teacher

Fear is often perceived as a negative emotion, but in small doses, it can actually be helpful. It can serve as a motivator to take action and prioritize safety. During the pandemic, fear of getting sick and transmitting the virus has compelled people to adopt protective measures such as wearing masks, practicing social distancing, and maintaining good hygiene. These actions have played a crucial role in mitigating the spread of the virus and safeguarding public health.

However, it is important to acknowledge that when fear becomes constant and overwhelming, it can have adverse effects on mental health. The prolonged state of fear and anxiety experienced during the pandemic has taken a toll on many individuals, leading to increased stress, depression, and other mental health challenges. It is crucial to address and manage these negative impacts by seeking support and practicing self-care.

One way to address the root of our fear is by not only naming the emotion but figuring out what caused us to be fearful in the first place. One way to do this in regard to the fear around COVID-19 is to pinpoint fear-mongering terms that became popular during the peak of the pandemic. Terms like "lockdown" and "social isolation" originate from the realm of prisons, where they are employed as punishments for wrongdoing. While the context is different in the current biosecurity situation, where the assumption is that everyone is potentially infectious until proven healthy, the usage of these terms can contribute to the framing of fear as a protective measure.

By critically evaluating the language and narratives surrounding our fears, we can gain a more nuanced perspective that allows us to separate rational concerns from exaggerated anxieties, enabling us to respond to the situation in a more balanced and measured manner. Understanding the origins of our fears empowers us to challenge and reframe them, ensuring that our responses align with the actual risks and realities we face.

Moreover, it is essential to seek accurate and reliable

information from credible sources. Misinformation and sensationalism can fuel fear and distort our perception of the situation. By staying informed through reputable channels, we can counteract the amplification of fear-inducing narratives and make informed decisions based on accurate data and expert guidance.

In doing so, we can strike a balance between acknowledging the legitimate risks associated with COVID-19 and maintaining a sense of perspective. It is crucial to approach our fears with rationality and discernment, understanding that excessive fear can hinder our ability to make sound judgments and impede our overall well-being if we neglect to use it as a teacher.

By addressing the root causes of our fears and ensuring they are grounded in evidence and rational assessment, we can navigate the challenges posed by the pandemic with resilience, determination, and a clearer understanding of the situation at hand.

It is essential to strike a balance between acknowledging the potential benefits of fear as a motivator for safety measures and recognizing the potential harm it can cause when it becomes excessive or chronic. By understanding and managing our fears, seeking appropriate support, and promoting a supportive and empathetic environment, we can navigate the challenges posed by the pandemic while safeguarding our mental well-being.

Fear is Normal

Fear is a natural and normal human emotion. It is a protective mechanism that helps us survive by keeping us alert to potential danger. Without fear, we would be vulnerable to harm and would not be able to make informed decisions to protect ourselves.

In ancient times, when our ancestors were hunters and gatherers, fear played a crucial role in their survival. Facing unpredictable and often dangerous environments, fear served as a valuable instinct that kept them vigilant and responsive to threats.

Imagine our ancestors navigating dense forests, tracking elusive prey, and encountering formidable predators. In these situations, fear triggered a cascade of physiological and psychological responses, sharpening their senses and preparing their bodies for fight or flight. It heightened their awareness and enabled them to assess risks, make split-second decisions, and take appropriate action to ensure their survival.

While the threats we face in modern times may differ significantly from those of our hunter-gatherer ancestors, the fundamental nature of fear remains unchanged. It is an innate response that continues to play a vital role in our lives. However, in the context of the COVID-19 pandemic, fear can become amplified and distorted due to the unprecedented scale and complexity of the crisis.

Recognizing the evolutionary origins of fear can provide us with a broader perspective. It allows us to acknowledge that fear, in its essence, is not inherently negative or detrimental. Instead, it is a normal survival tool that is actually meant to protect us from harm.

The COVID-19 pandemic has brought about numerous liminal moments for many people around the world. The sudden outbreak of the virus, coupled with the subsequent lockdowns, travel restrictions, and economic downturns, has created a sense of uncertainty and fear for many individuals.

The pandemic has been an unprecedented crisis, and it's normal to feel fear in such situations. In fact, it would be abnormal *not* to feel fear. It is important to acknowledge and validate our feelings of fear rather than suppress them. Instead of beating ourselves up and succumbing to paranoid feelings fueled by fear, we need to be understanding and resilient. We need to seek out support and resources to help us navigate this difficult time. We can also learn from the experiences of others and share our own stories to create a sense of community and a space for collective action.

By recognizing and embracing our fears, we can better understand ourselves and find ways to cope with the challenges that come with living through a pandemic. It is important to remember that fear is a part of our humanity, and it does not define us as people. We can learn to coexist with our fears and find strength in our ability to adapt and overcome.

Truth is Fragile

Fear and the fragility of truth related to COVID-19 are intertwined in a way that they can reinforce each other. Fear can make people more susceptible to misinformation and conspiracy theories, which, in turn, erode trust in scientific evidence and public health messaging. This creates a vicious cycle where people become increasingly fearful and skeptical, making it harder to communicate accurate information and implement effective public health measures.

As author Laura Dodsworth asserts, as we recover from an epidemic, we must also restore the trust and transparency that we deserve. During the COVID-19 pandemic, there has been a surge in misinformation and fake news, which is a serious problem. False information can lead to poor decision-making with significant consequences for people's health. In the face of uncertainty, it is crucial to avoid falling into the trap of misinformation and falsehoods. To combat this, it is essential to seek reliable sources of information, fact-check everything before acting upon it, and be mindful of the potential biases and agendas of the sources we consume.

Fear permeates various aspects of the pandemic, such as fear of the virus, fear of death, fear of change, fear of the unknown, fear of ulterior motives, agendas, and conspiracies, fear for the rule of law, democracy, and the Western liberal way of life, and fear of loss in multiple domains. The government's utilization of fear as a weapon is also a significant concern.

While some may argue that fear is useful, it is also easily manipulated and exploited. There is a fine line between productive fear and unproductive fear. Considering the future of truth in a world inundated with misinformation, fake news, and propaganda, it becomes crucial to address the concept of fear. In the age of the internet, discerning fact from fiction has become increasingly challenging, as evidenced by the selection of words like "post-truth" and "misinformation" as words of the year by reputable dictionaries. Predictions of a "nuclear winter of misinformation" pose a serious threat to democratic institutions. However, amidst the challenges lies an opportunity for growth and learning. The early days of the pandemic and social distancing efforts have demonstrated fear's power as a teacher. The current crisis can be viewed as a chance to enhance our ability to differentiate truth from falsehood, develop critical thinking skills, and increase awareness of our biases and the agendas of those who propagate misinformation. That way, we can make sure our fear matches the reality of the situation and is justified. From there, we can use it to guide our decision-making.

We Had a Double Pandemic

"We're not just fighting a pandemic; we're fighting an infodemic," said Tedros Adhanom Ghebreyesus, WHO's director-general, at the 2020 Munich Security Conference. Fake news, misinformation, and conspiracy theories have become prevalent in the age of social media and have skyrocketed since the beginning of the COVID-19 pandemic. This situation is extremely concerning because it undermines trust in health institutions and programs. Remember the early and eerie days of COVID-19 when the media posted a picture of emergency staff in protective suits checking the body of a man who collapsed and died in the street in Wuhan, or overcrowded ICU hospitals in Italy? Nothing fuels fear and anxiety like uncertainty. With the ever-increasing use of social media, the infodemic was wreaking havoc even before the pandemic. There is a wealth of research on the spread of fake news, including a recent study from MIT that shows false news travels faster than true stories. In their research project, the team finds that it is not bots but humans who are primarily responsible for spreading misleading information.

Why Misinformation Exists?

During the early days of the pandemic, fear was extensively used by governments and various media channels. Although it was not a coordinated effort, echoing Machiavelli's suggestion to young leaders, it is considered safer to be feared than loved because love is preserved by the link of obligation, which, owing to the baseness of men, is broken at every opportunity for their advantage. However, fear preserves you through a dread of punishment that never fails.

Let's reflect on our recent memories. We were told that the US or Chinese government created this virus, that it was the master plan of Bill Gates, and that the virus spread via 5G towers. While some of these claims were absurd, others appeared so real that many people became ineffective at detecting fake news because it often resembled genuine news.

Whether misinformation arises from good or bad intentions, it exists because we live in a decentralized world. As Ben Thompson mentioned earlier in 2022, it is part of a broader trend of unbundling in media. With the waves of unbundling, we have become more susceptible to post-truth. But what exactly *is* truth?

Science of Truth Making

I remember having a conversation with a friend of mine. We were debating over the definition of truth. While it is definitely not what it is for many people the truth is the first search result they find in their Google search. As Aldous Huxley said, "Facts do not cease to exist because they are ignored." So, how can we find the truth?

To fight back against misinformation, here are two key tips:

Check your sources: Ensure that you are getting information from reputable sources. Before sharing something, take a few minutes to do a quick fact-check.

Think before you share: Just because something is popular or trending doesn't mean it's true. Before sharing something, ask yourself if it seems credible. If you're unsure, it's best not to share it.

By following these two tips, you can help combat the spread of misinformation and fake news. In turn, any fears that you do have will be more rational and not caused by misinformation, but by the reality of an objectively stressful yet manageable situation.

However, the prevalence of fake news during the pandemic highlights the increasing fragility of the truth. With the rise of the internet, misinformation can spread more easily than ever before. In today's political climate and the rise of AI-generated deep fake content, it is crucial to be able to distinguish between fact and fiction.

Be Skeptical of Everything You Read, See, or Hear

For many of us, the first search result on Google is often considered the truth. In fact, Google does not provide us with the answer or the truth directly; it simply presents us with what other individuals have expressed as the truth. That is why, just because something is on the internet doesn't mean it's true. It's important to take the time to check multiple sources and verify the information before believing anything you read. This will help you avoid falling victim to false information that could be harmful to your health and well-being.

It's also important to question everything. When you come across something that raises doubts about its truthfulness, take the time to conduct research and seek answers. Don't believe something solely because someone else said it. It's crucial to be proactive in seeking accurate and reliable information and to question any information that appears false or misleading.

As we explored in the previous chapter mental models play a significant role in our fight against misinformation. Mental models are simplified representations of complex systems or phenomena that help us make sense of the world around us. They serve as cognitive shortcuts to process information and make decisions. One mental model that aids skepticism and encourages questioning is Occam's Razor.

Occam's Razor suggests that when faced with multiple explanations, we should choose the simplest one that aligns with the available evidence. It is often expressed as "entities should not be multiplied unnecessarily." By avoiding unnecessary complexity in our explanations and favoring simpler ones when feasible, we can apply Occam's Razor as a mental model to combat misinformation and complexities that we face in our operation.

This will also make us confident in the fact that our fears if we have any, are aligned with reality and not false truths. By employing Occam's Razor and opting for the simplest explanation supported by evidence, we can avoid being deceived by complex and convoluted explanations that may be designed to mislead.

In conclusion, even before the COVID-19 pandemic, we were already navigating uncharted territory in the realm of post-truth. The pandemic further highlighted the fragility and relativity of truth and how its absence fuels fear fueled by fake news. Nonetheless, the pandemic also demonstrated the importance of tracing information sources and adopting a critical perspective to restore truth and alleviate the collective hysteria triggered by the post-truth era. In the age of climate anxiety, it is crucial to distinguish between fact and fiction and concentrate on the systems we operate within as Capra suggests in his systemic view. While fear can serve as a teacher and is a normal emotion, we should not allow it to dominate our actions. It has become evident during the pandemic that the apocalyptic scenarios portrayed by many media companies are less likely to occur than commonly narrated. Similarly, the narrative of a climate apocalypse, running out of time, last generation, or saving the planet from destruction should be approached with caution. Life on Earth will continue, even if our species were to disappear. Instead of working against nature, it is time to focus on building for the planet.

Whether you are a founder or a business leader, it is likely that fear and anxiety might haunt you. As Lao Tzu said, *"The named is the mother of myriad things."* Defining our emotions, and the source of them can help us to overcome the numerous challenges they bring, including the climate crisis.

CHAPTER 3: THE DAY WORLD STANDS STILL

When the World Health Organization (WHO) declared COVID-19 a pandemic, it marked a watershed moment that would forever change the history of humanity. It was a day when our familiar way of life underwent an irrevocable transformation. In the year 2020, a global pandemic took hold, originating in China and swiftly spreading its grip across the globe within a matter of months.

In those initial days, uncertainty and fear permeated society. As the number of confirmed cases and fatalities continued to escalate, anxiety and fear took over. The media inundated us with distressing images of overwhelmed hospitals and heartrending stories of personal loss. The world seemed to grind to a halt, leaving people apprehensive and confined within their homes. Governments scrambled to react to this crisis, while the medical community labored tirelessly in pursuit of a cure. Suddenly, our world became an entirely different place.

Yet, amidst the prevailing fear and uncertainty, a remarkable spirit of solidarity emerged. Neighbors extended their support to one another, volunteers tirelessly delivered essential supplies to those in need, and individuals endeavored to sustain the economy through any means possible. It was a period of immense challenge in many fronts, but it was also a time that showcased our species' extraordinary resilience and unwavering hope.

As time progressed, the world gradually began its journey toward recovery. Following the initial waves, at a great speed, vaccines were developed, and the number of cases began to decline. Slowly but surely, the world and economies reopened, allowing people to resume their work and education. This was a difficult and extended process, but one that ultimately brought individuals closer together and illuminated the intrinsic value of life's most vital aspects.

However, these challenges triggered an unparalleled disruption worldwide, leading to a standstill in global economic activities. Many founders, businesses and industries shuttered their operations in response to social distancing measures, exposing the fragility of our economic systems. Nevertheless, this pause offered an opportunity to introspect, reflect, and reshape our organizations. In this chapter, we delve into the invaluable lessons learned from the interruption of economic activities during the pandemic.

The pandemic has underscored the critical importance of resilience and adaptability in the face of crisis. It has also emphasized the urgent need to prioritize sustainability and social well-being over short-term gains. The pause in economic activities throughout the pandemic has bestowed upon us a chance to reflect upon our practices and embrace new approaches that are more sustainable, equitable, and resilient.

Let's explore the profound transformations and insights that have emerged from the temporary cessation of economic activities during this unprecedented global crisis. By exploring these insights, we can improve our impact, design better business models, become more adaptable, and stay resilient in times of unexpected change.

ABC of Pivoting: Need for Time and Space to Reflect on Complex Challenges

The COVID-19 pandemic has been a defining moment in the history of humanity, bringing the world to a standstill. The suddenness and magnitude of the crisis forced individuals, communities, and nations to confront complex challenges that were previously ignored or deemed too difficult to address. The first lesson from this crisis is the need for time and space to reflect on these challenges.

The term "polycrisis," coined in the 1970s and popularized by historian Adam Tooze, refers to the interaction of multiple crises occurring simultaneously. The pandemic, when combined with the ongoing climate crisis, has amplified the scale and scope of the complex challenges we face. These crises demonstrate that change is an inherent part of our lives and that we must adapt and respond accordingly. Confucius's suggestion of self-reflection and introspection becomes particularly relevant in the face of this constant and inevitable change. Engaging in mindfulness and introspective practices allows us founders to navigate these challenges more effectively. By taking time to contemplate our actions and decisions, we gain a deeper understanding of their impact on the world around us. This self-reflection helps us identify areas where change is necessary and opportunities for improving our practices.

For businesses and startups, embracing the idea of change as the only constant requires a step back and evaluation of their impact on the environment and society. The pandemic-induced pause in economic activities offers a valuable moment for businesses to reflect on various aspects of their operations. This includes examining their supply chains, energy usage, and waste management practices. By engaging in this introspective process, businesses can identify areas where they can make meaningful changes and adopt more sustainable practices.

One of the useful tools and areas that I've built my practice is impact modeling and management. While these concepts are used mostly for the non-profit sectors, with the pandemic the importance of impact modeling became more relevant, not only because the need is ever relevant but because more and more founders wanted to build something for the planet.

By embracing reflection and integrating impact modeling and management into their practices, businesses can embark on a transformative journey toward sustainability and regeneration. They can proactively address their environmental footprint, enhance social well-being, and optimize their contributions to society. Sir Ronald Cohen in his Impact Revolution approach says that impact must be embedded in our society's DNA, part of a triple helix of risk–return–impact that influences every decision we make regarding consumption, employment, business and investment. It needs to become a driving force of our economy.

As we navigate the aftermath of the pandemic and strive to rebuild a more resilient world, the lessons derived from the pause in economic activities during this crisis resonate profoundly. Let us seize this pivotal moment to engage in reflection, adopt sustainable practices, and contribute to a future that balances the imperatives of profit, people, and the planet.

Wayfinding and Impact Modeling

One of the key ways in which businesses can evaluate their practices is through impact modeling. Impact modeling involves analyzing the social, environmental, and economic impact of a business. This analysis can help businesses identify areas where they can make improvements and adopt more sustainable practices.

The COVID-19 pandemic has emphasized the crucial role of impact modeling, as businesses have had to swiftly adapt their practices to address the unprecedented challenges it has presented. For instance, disruptions in supply chains and logistics due to the pandemic forced businesses to reevaluate their approaches. Impact modeling offers a valuable framework for identifying vulnerabilities within the supply chain and taking proactive steps to mitigate risks. By scrutinizing various aspects of the supply chain, such as sourcing, transportation, and inventory management, businesses can identify potential bottlenecks and develop contingency plans to minimize disruption and ensure the resilience of their operations.

Moreover, impact modeling plays a pivotal role in evaluating the social impact of business practices. More often, social and environmental impact are seen from public relations side but in reality impact models can provide strategic insights for the companies. Through impact modeling, businesses can meticulously assess their existing practices and policies, identifying areas where additional support can be provided to employees. This may include initiatives to enhance work-life balance, foster a positive and inclusive work environment, and promote employee well-being through mental health resources and support networks. By utilizing impact modeling to address these vital social aspects, businesses can cultivate a motivated and resilient workforce while contributing to the overall welfare of their employees.

Furthermore, impact modeling offers businesses a comprehensive framework to assess their environmental impact and adopt more sustainable practices. The pandemic has amplified the urgency of addressing climate crisis and resource depletion. By conducting a meticulous analysis of energy usage, waste management, and carbon emissions, businesses can identify areas where they can reduce their environmental footprint. This may involve implementing energy-efficient technologies, adopting circular economy principles, or investing in renewable energy sources. Impact modeling enables businesses to make informed decisions regarding sustainability practices, fostering a harmonious relationship between economic prosperity and environmental stewardship. Let's not forget, every business has a positive and negative impact, by knowing our impact, we can adopt a do-no-harm strategy to minimize the unintended negative impact of our products and services.

Pivoting is Easier

Another way in which the pandemic has made businesses evaluate their business models is through business model pivoting. Business model pivoting involves making significant changes to a business model in response to changing circumstances or new opportunities.

The pandemic has forced businesses to reconsider their existing business models and look for new opportunities. For example, many businesses have shifted their focus to online sales and e-commerce in response to the closure of physical stores. Other businesses have adapted their products or services to meet changing customer needs, such as producing personal protective equipment (PPE) or hand sanitizer.

Business model pivoting can be challenging, as it requires significant changes to a business's operations and strategy. However, businesses that are able to pivot successfully can emerge from the pandemic with a more resilient and sustainable business model. Those who fail to do this will be left behind in the face of unprecedented change.

Recognizing the complex challenges posed by global sustainable development goals is not only crucial from a societal and environmental standpoint but also holds immense potential as a business opportunity. While discussions around impact modeling and business model pivoting might evoke notions of philanthropy, it is important to emphasize the pragmatism inherent in these approaches. By aligning business practices with impact and sustainability, companies can tap into a vast market and address the substantial funding gap that exists.

The funding gap required to meet the sustainable development goals currently stands at an astonishing $4 trillion USD. This figure highlights the scale of investment needed to propel progress toward a sustainable future (UNDP, 2020). Astonishingly, developing countries alone allocate approximately $1.4 trillion annually towards the 17 goals and 169 targets, with about $360 billion contributed by low-income countries and approximately $940 billion by middle and lower-income countries (UNDP, 2020)[7]. These statistics underscore the existing expenditure and market potential within these regions that remain underserved not due to a lack of profitability but often due to their exclusion as priority customers.

However, by reframing the traditional profit-driven mindset and incorporating impact considerations,

---

[7] https://unstats.un.org/sdgs/report/2020/The-Sustainable-Development-Goals-Report-2020.pdf

businesses can forge new models that not only yield profitability but also benefit people and build for planet. This paradigm shift represents an opportunity to unlock the potential of these markets and deliver sustainable solutions. By integrating impact modeling into their strategic decision-making, businesses can identify untapped market segments, unmet needs, and opportunities to address social and environmental challenges.

Regenerative business models are gaining traction as a worthwhile avenue to explore in this context. These models emphasize not just sustainability, but the restoration and enhancement of ecological and social systems. To transition to a regenerative business model, the initial step involves a shift in mindset. According to co-founder of Regenesis Group Bill Reed, altering our perspective is the first essential aspect of embarking on the journey towards regenerative work. They highlight the significance of this transformation, emphasizing that it encompasses more than simply adopting a few new ways of thinking. Instead, it entails embracing an entirely different mindset, one that embraces a distinct worldview and approaches the world from a contrasting paradigm. By adopting regenerative practices, businesses can go beyond mitigating their negative impacts and actively contribute to the restoration of ecosystems and the well-being of communities. This approach fosters a symbiotic relationship where profitability and positive impact go hand in hand, creating a virtuous cycle that benefits all stakeholders involved.

The Leverage of the Degrowth Business Models

The COVID-19 pandemic highlighted the unsustainability of the existing economic system, which prioritizes growth and profits over the health and well-being of people and the planet which is also known as Milton Friedman's doctrine. Another lesson from this crisis is the need to create viable degrowth business models that prioritize sustainability, resilience, and regeneration.

Degrowth is a movement that seeks to create a society that is less focused on economic growth and more focused on sustainability, equality, and well-being. Degrowth business models prioritize local production, circular economies, and the use of renewable resources. They also prioritize the health and well-being of workers, customers, and communities.

A degrowth business model is based on the following principles:

- Sufficiency: Focus on meeting basic needs and enhancing well-being rather than endless consumption.
- Localization: Prioritize local production and consumption to reduce transportation and energy use and build community resilience.
- Circular economy: Design products and services for reuse, recycling, and regeneration to reduce waste and resource depletion.
- Commons-based peer production: Encourage collaborative and open-source approaches to knowledge, innovation, and governance to promote sustainability and social justice while also thinking about the upcoming generations.

With the ever increasing global temperatures, increasing likelihood of drought and exhausting natural resources, ventures that promote regeneration and degrowth will be praised by the market. This will be a leverage of the next generation of founders.

Strategies for Creating Viable Degrowth Enterprises

Melanie Rieback, the founder of the Post Growth Entrepreneurship (PGE) Incubator, argues that a significant portion of the startup ecosystem tends to adopt the Silicon Valley approach of "capital, scale, exit." In contrast, Rieback advocates for a different approach, which involves bootstrapping, pursuing sustainable and manageable growth, and avoiding practices that deplete resources or extract value without replenishment. Creating a viable degrowth enterprise requires a combination of innovative thinking, entrepreneurship, and collaboration. Here are some strategies for achieving this goal:

- Start small: Begin with a modest venture that aligns with the principles of degrowth, such as a local food cooperative, a repair café, or a shared workspace.
- Collaborate: Seek partnerships and alliances with other degrowth enterprises, community organizations, and social movements to build a network of mutual support and solidarity.
- Be innovative: Experiment with new business models, such as product-service systems, sharing

platforms, or worker cooperatives, that promote sufficiency, localization, and circular economy.

- Embrace transparency: Be transparent about your business practices, including your social and environmental impact, and engage with stakeholders to co-create solutions.

- Advocate for policy change: Lobby for policy changes that support degrowth principles, such as local procurement, eco-taxes, and basic income, and challenge policies that promote growth at all costs.

Examples of Degrowth Business Models:

There are many examples of degrowth business models that demonstrate the potential for sustainable and equitable enterprise. Here are a few:

- The Share Shed: A community tool library in Totnes, UK, that provides access to tools and equipment for gardening, DIY, and maintenance, reducing the need for individual ownership and promoting sharing.

- Rizome: A worker-owned cooperative in Barcelona, Spain, that offers organic and local food, ecological cleaning products, and social and cultural activities, promoting sufficiency and localization.

- Repair Café: A global movement of repair workshops where volunteers help people fix their broken appliances, clothing, and electronics, reducing waste and promoting a circular economy.

- Enercoop: A French cooperative that offers 100% renewable energy and promotes citizen participation in the energy transition, challenging the dominance of fossil fuel-based corporations.

5. Radically Open Security: Amsterdam based ROS is the world's first non-profit computer security consultancy company. As with the pandemic, there is an increasing appetite and need for regenerative businesses. Degrowth business models offer a compelling alternative to the unsustainable and unequal growth-based economy. By prioritizing sufficiency, localization, circular economy, and commons-based peer production, degrowth enterprises can promote sustainability, resilience, and regeneration.

COVID-19 has shown us that degrowth business models

are not only desirable but essential. The pandemic disrupted global supply chains, exposed the vulnerability of globalized production systems, and highlighted the importance of local resilience. It also showed us that a focus on growth at all costs can lead to social and environmental crises. According to economist Branko Milanovic, although GDP is imperfect, it provides a general understanding of a country's well-being. Richer countries tend to excel in education, healthcare, and happiness. Degrowth-related concerns like leisure time, healthcare, and life expectancy are associated with societal wealth, as are innovation and support for the poorest. In essence, Milanovic suggests that the objectives of degrowth align with the advantages of a wealthier society. The examples of existing degrowth business models serve as powerful illustrations of the potential for enterprises that prioritize the well-being of people and the planet. However, achieving this transformation requires a significant course correction in our societal and economic systems.

Following E. F. Schumacher's motto of "small is beautiful" to create viable degrowth ventures, it becomes evident that we need to adopt a different approach. To effectively transition towards degrowth business models, we must start small, collaborate with like-minded organizations, foster innovation, embrace transparency, and advocate for broader systems change. It is through these collective efforts that we can challenge the prevailing growth paradigm and steer our economies toward more sustainable and equitable pathways.

The Essentials of Course Correction

Course correction for entrepreneurs involves proactively adjusting the direction, strategy, or actions of their ventures based on new information, market conditions, or unexpected challenges. It requires monitoring progress, recognizing signals for change, being flexible and adaptable, seeking feedback, and maintaining a long-term vision. For our liminal times, the COVID-19 pandemic has been a wake-up call for humanity. It has highlighted the need for a course correction in our society, economy, and governance. Another lesson from the pandemic is the need to identify the essentials of course correction. Just like impact modeling, a practice of course correction is a critical aspect of managing organizations and programs. It helps to determine whether they are achieving their intended outcomes and whether they are making a positive impact on society. The essential aspects of course correction must be identified and measured to ensure that we are on the right track.

As a practice of course correction, measuring the impact of an organization or program is crucial for several reasons. First, it helps to determine whether the intended outcomes are being achieved. Second, it helps to identify areas that need improvement. Third, it provides accountability to stakeholders, including funders, clients, and beneficiaries. Last, but not least, it helps to identify the most effective approaches and strategies to achieve the intended outcomes while minimizing the negative impact.

Measuring the impact of our products and services is essential for course correction. However, measuring impact can be challenging, and there are different methods and tools available. Some of the common methods include:

- *Outcome measurement:* Outcome measurement involves assessing the impact of a program or policy on its intended outcomes. This can be done through surveys, interviews, or other methods to collect data from beneficiaries or stakeholders.
- *Social Return on Investment (SROI):* SROI is a method that measures the social, environmental,

and economic impact of a program or policy. It calculates the return on investment in terms of the value created for society, including financial returns and non-financial benefits.

- *Stakeholder Mapping:* Stakeholder mapping, from a founder's perspective, is a strategic process of identifying and understanding the individuals, groups, or organizations that have a vested interest or impact on the success of their venture. By recognizing and analyzing these stakeholders, founders can effectively engage and manage relationships to drive positive outcomes, align their business goals with stakeholder expectations, and enhance the overall impact of their startup.

The COVID-19 pandemic has had a profound impact on businesses all over the world. However, it also provided a much-needed space for slowing down. The pause in economic activities has given businesses an opportunity to reflect on their practices and evaluate their business models. Impact modeling and self-reflection are two key ways in which businesses have evaluated their practices for a pivot for planet during the pandemic.

Impact modeling, management, and measurement can

help businesses identify areas where they can make improvements and adopt more sustainable practices. By analyzing the social, environmental, and economic impact of their practices, businesses can identify areas where they can reduce their environmental impact, improve working conditions, and support their communities. While this is quite essential, my experience with many acceleration programs show that it is often not prioritized by founders.

Just as Eliel Saarinen emphasized the importance of viewing objects or spaces within their larger context, we must understand how individual elements fit into the larger whole and how they interact with their surroundings. This principle holds true not only for architecture and design but also for our approach to business and life in general.

The slowdowns experienced during the pandemic have given us an opportunity to pause, reflect, and gain a deeper understanding of the world around us. By embracing this notion of slowdown, as suggested by Zen Buddhist Haemin Sunim, we can uncover insights and discover things that can only be seen when we take the time to observe and reflect.

Ultimately, as founders, let us heed the lessons of the pandemic, embrace the principles of self-reflection, slowdown, and holistic understanding, and strive to create ventures that not only succeed economically but also align with the well-being of individuals, communities, and the planet. In doing so, we can shape a future that values quality over quantity, purpose over profit, and harmony with the world around us.

CHAPTER 4: COLLECTIVE ACTION AND SOCIAL DISTANCING

The outbreak of COVID-19 caused a global halt, with social distancing emerging as a vital strategy in combating the virus. From then on, people had to reduce close contact with others. The concept of social distancing was not new, but it was the first time in modern history that it was implemented on a global scale.

During the initial stages of the pandemic, the implementation of social distancing measures was marked by inconsistency and disarray. Governments faced significant challenges in coordinating their efforts, leading to a lack of unified response. The medical community was confronted with an unprecedented influx of cases, pushing healthcare systems to their limits. People were afraid, and the world felt like it was coming apart at the seams.

However, as the pandemic progressed, the importance of social distancing became clearer. Governments and health organizations around the world began to coordinate their efforts and implement consistent social distancing measures. The world slowly began to understand the crucial role of social distancing in the fight against the virus.

Collective action was also critical in the progress of social distancing. On top of the fact that the majority of people began social distancing, people also came together to help each other, and communities worked to keep their economies going in any way they could. It was a time of immense challenge, but also a time of great hope and resilience. The progress of social distancing was a testament to the power of collective action and the role that it played in overcoming the pandemic. Popularized by Stanford Social Innovation Review, the term collective impact requires all stakeholders to have a shared vision for change and mutually reinforcing activities. During the pandemic, we have utilized this tool to flatten the curve. Let's see how collective action can help founders who are building for planet.

Usually, as venture builders, we ship a product or build a company when we found a problem that we can solve efficiently. While in business as usual, the problems of the customers can be solved by a single player, in the time of poly-crisis, we have realized that planetary problems cannot be solved by a single actor. As Lyndon

B. Johnson said, "There are no problems we cannot solve together, and very few that we can solve by ourselves." That is why we need collective action in the impact entrepreneurship ecosystems. For founders, social innovation holds significant importance, especially in times of crisis like the COVID-19 pandemic. It's worth noting that collective action during the pandemic extended beyond individual efforts and took shape on a global scale. A remarkable illustration of this was the organization of numerous global hackathons aimed at finding solutions to the challenges posed by the pandemic. As someone involved in local organizing for collective thinking events, these hackathons brought together experts from diverse fields such as technology, medicine, and public health. Their collaboration aimed to discover novel approaches to combat the pandemic. One standout example was the Global Hack, recognized as the world's largest online hackathon. It witnessed the participation of over 100,000 individuals from all corners of the globe, united in their efforts to address COVID-19.

The outcomes were truly remarkable. These hackathons yielded a range of innovative solutions, including advancements in contact tracing technologies, the creation of online resources for remote learning, and the development of enhanced communication and collaboration tools for healthcare professionals. They vividly demonstrated the power of collective action and the profound impact it can have during times of crisis. The success of these hackathons also showcased the potential of social innovation to drive positive change, fostering a sense of hope and resilience in the face of adversity.

Since the early days of COVID-19, collective action has proven to be a powerful tool in addressing global challenges, and it can continue to play a crucial role in tackling future challenges as well. Here are a few ways in which collective action can be used to address upcoming global challenges in the age of polycrisis:

1. Climate crisis: Climate change is one of the biggest challenges facing the world today, and it requires collective action on a global scale to address it. Governments, organizations, and individuals need to work together to reduce greenhouse gas emissions, increase the use of renewable energy, and implement sustainable practices.

2. Global health crisis: The COVID-19 pandemic has highlighted the importance of collective action in addressing global health crises. By working together, governments, organizations, and individuals can pool resources, share information, and collaborate on

developing and distributing effective treatments and vaccines.

3. Economic inequality: Economic inequality is a growing problem in many countries, requiring collective action to address it. Governments, organizations, and individuals need to work together to ensure that everyone has access to opportunities for education, employment, and economic growth.

As Fabian Pfortmueller from Together Institute said relationships are a tremendous and highly under-leveraged source of transformation and wellbeing. Things, services, offerings, and systems simply become better when we design them in a relational way. By coming together as communities, we as founders can pool our resources, share our expertise, and collaborate on finding solutions. The impact of collective action can be far-reaching and long-lasting, and it is essential for addressing the complex and interrelated challenges facing the world today and in the age of poly-crisis.

The Climate Crisis Has an Attention Problem

Just as collective action during the COVID-19 pandemic showcased the power of collaboration and innovation, a similar approach is necessary for combating the climate crisis. This issue's interconnected and global nature calls for the mobilization of collective efforts, where individuals, communities, organizations, and governments unite to tackle the complex challenges at hand. It requires a collective shift in priorities, increased awareness, and widespread engagement to drive meaningful change and implement sustainable solutions that are required to regenerate the natural resources and biodiversity.

Although the climate crisis is one of the most pressing issues facing humanity today, it continues to be met with a significant attention deficit. Despite its gravity and the mounting evidence of its devastating effects, the issue of climate change remains largely absent from the public discourse, media coverage, and political agenda. The attention deficiency problem is a critical obstacle to addressing the climate crisis effectively, and it requires urgent attention.

There are several reasons why climate change has an attention deficiency problem. First, the issue is complex and multifaceted, making it difficult for individuals to comprehend fully. Climate change involves complex scientific concepts, intricate economic models, and political dimensions that are challenging to grasp, particularly for non-experts. The complexity of the issue can lead to information overload, confusion, and a sense of helplessness, making it challenging to motivate people to take action.

Second, the gradual and often invisible nature of the effects of climate change presents another challenge. Unlike natural disasters such as earthquakes or hurricanes, the impacts of climate change are gradual, incremental, and often indirect. They may take years or even decades to manifest themselves and may not be immediately visible to people living in affected areas. This gradual and invisible nature of climate change can make it challenging to motivate people to take action as the sense of urgency may not be as apparent.

Third, the media's tendency to focus on individual rather than systemic solutions further exacerbates the attention deficiency problem. The media tends to frame the issue of climate change as an individual lifestyle choice, such as driving an electric car or reducing meat consumption. While individual choices can make a difference, they are not sufficient to address the systemic causes of climate change. Focusing on individual choices can also create a sense of guilt and blame among individuals who feel powerless to address the issue effectively.

Finally, the attention deficiency problem is also related to the pervasive influence of vested interests, particularly in the fossil fuel industry, which has a significant financial stake in maintaining the status quo. The fossil fuel industry has employed a range of tactics, such as lobbying, funding climate-denying think tanks, and creating doubt about the scientific consensus on climate change, to influence public opinion and policy decisions. The influence of vested interests can create a sense of confusion and mistrust, making it difficult to build momentum for collective action when it comes to combating climate change.

To address the attention deficiency problem effectively, it is crucial to shift the narrative towards a broader understanding of the climate crisis as a multifaceted issue that requires systemic solutions. This involves highlighting the responsibility of large corporations, governments, and institutions in driving sustainable practices, transitioning to renewable energy sources, and implementing policies that reduce greenhouse gas emissions. By directing attention to these systemic factors, individuals can feel empowered to advocate for change on a larger scale and hold the appropriate entities accountable for their environmental impact.

Encouraging a more comprehensive and nuanced discussion surrounding the climate crisis is vital to foster a collective sense of responsibility and facilitating the necessary systemic changes. By redirecting blame from individuals to the larger actors shaping the trajectory of climate change, society can mobilize collective action, influence policy decisions, and drive transformative shifts toward a sustainable future.

The attention deficiency problem surrounding the climate crisis is a critical obstacle that must be overcome to address this urgent issue effectively. To do so, we need to focus on better communication and education, shift the media's framing of the issue, and implement policy change that prioritizes climate action. We can also look to the business case for transitioning away from fossil fuels, as well as the potential benefits to health, quality of life, and the economy, to create a more compelling case for action.

One significant factor that could help increase attention to the climate crisis is the growing awareness that the global geopolitical landscape is being shaped by fossil fuel interests. Russian oil and gas companies, for example, are using their energy reserves to wield influence over countries in their sphere of influence, while countries like the United States and China are increasingly competing for control over energy resources. The impact of these dynamics on the environment, as well as global stability, is profound and underscores the urgency of transitioning to renewable energy sources.

One way to create attention and urgency around the issue of climate change is to highlight the benefits of collective action. The example of the closing of the ozone layer is instructive in this regard. In the 1980s, a gaping hole in the ozone layer over the Antarctic was discovered, caused by the use of ozone-depleting chemicals such as chlorofluorocarbons (CFCs) in refrigerators and air conditioners. Thanks to international cooperation and collective action, a treaty was signed in 1987 to phase out the use of these chemicals. By 2019, the ozone hole had shrunk by 1.5 million square miles, demonstrating the power of collective action in addressing these complex problems.

All in all, the attention deficiency problem surrounding the climate crisis requires urgent action. We need to prioritize communication, education, policy change, and collective action to address the systemic causes of climate change. Recognizing the power of collective action in solving complex problems is not exclusive to the climate crisis; it has also proven instrumental in addressing other global challenges. One striking illustration of this is the role of collective intelligence and collaborative efforts in combating the COVID-19 pandemic. With the virus spreading rapidly across the globe, it has become evident that a unified and cooperative approach is crucial in devising innovative solutions to effectively tackle the pandemic's challenges.

Role of Collective Action in Solving Complex Problems

As articulated by Gerd Trogemann: "No matter how well conceived and relevant in their own right, projects tend to pursue single point rather than systemic solutions, limit strategic space and the ability to adapt continuously and to connect the dots systemically. Systemic solutions need adaptive ways of working, strategic space, iterative learning, and radical collaboration. With the rapid spread of the virus across the world, it has become clear that a collaborative effort is essential in developing innovative solutions that can effectively address the challenges brought about by the pandemic. In this context, the European Commission, in partnership with the European Innovation Council and EU member states, organized a Pan-European Matchathon. This initiative aimed to leverage the collective intelligence of individuals from various sectors, bringing together civil society, innovators, partners, and investors, to develop innovative solutions for coronavirus-related challenges. The event saw an impressive turnout of over 30,000 participants from the EU and beyond, who submitted more than 2,164 projects in different domains.

The COVID-19 pandemic has also highlighted the importance of collective action in addressing the climate crisis. Many of the measures put in place to control the spread of the virus have had positive environmental effects, such as reduced air pollution and lower greenhouse gas emissions. This has underscored the potential for collective action to address the root causes of the climate crisis, including the reliance on fossil fuels and the lack of political will to transition to renewable energy sources. With all these changes and impact one thing became clear: For a better future, our direction for collective action should not be sustaining what it is but regenerating what is next to come.

By definition acting on climate change is a collective action problem. This is when the optimal total outcome requires collaboration, but due to the incentives of individual actors, a suboptimal path is taken. However, from a systemic perspective, building for planet is the right thing to do as the markets are finally rewarding solutions for solving climate problems. In 2022, climate tech saw record-breaking levels of investment, even higher than its impressive performance in 2021.

Climate Tech is a term used to describe technology that helps address the problem of climate crisis whether used in mitigation e.g. to help reduce greenhouse gas emissions, like renewable energy technologies and electric vehicles, or adaptation to help the planet in adapting to the changing climate, such as crops resistant to drought and buildings that can withstand floods. As technology continues to disrupt and change traditional industries, nature has yet to experience the full impact of technological disruption.

As the world transitions from sustainability to regeneration, from high-tech to low-tech, climate tech companies have a unique opportunity to solve multiple problems facing our planet. During the COVID lockdown periods, many individuals and communities have taken collective action to reduce their environmental footprint and promote sustainability. For example, people have been cycling or walking instead of driving, reducing their energy consumption, and increasing their use of renewable energy sources. Communities have also taken collective action by implementing green infrastructure, such as community gardens, rooftop gardens, and green roofs, to promote local food production and reduce the urban heat island effect.

Another example of collective action during the COVID lockdown periods is the growth of community-led initiatives focused on sustainability and environmental stewardship. For example, many communities have created mutual aid networks to support vulnerable members of society during the pandemic. These networks have also been used to share resources and knowledge about sustainability and promote environmentally-friendly practices.

Finally, the COVID lockdown periods have highlighted the importance of collective action in advocating for policy change. During the pandemic, many individuals and organizations have called for a green recovery that prioritizes sustainability and regeneration.

In conclusion, the examples of the COVID-19 pandemic and the climate crisis underscore the transformative power of collective action in addressing complex problems in the age of poly-crisis. The success of such collective acts leading to positive social and environmental impact showcases the value of collective efforts in solving complex problems that our society faces.

These examples of collective action in the face of the COVID-19 pandemic and the climate crisis highlight the immense potential it holds to shape a better world for ourselves and future generations. By leveraging the power of collaboration, collective intelligence, and shared responsibility, we can forge a path toward a more sustainable, equitable, and resilient future.

However, it is crucial to acknowledge that collective action requires ongoing commitment, active participation, and collaboration across diverse stakeholders. Building bridges, fostering dialogue, and creating platforms for collaboration are key to mobilizing collective action effectively. By amplifying the voices of individuals, communities, and organizations, we can create a collective movement that drives sustainable practices, influences policy decisions, and addresses the systemic causes of global challenges.

Ultimately, as a type of social innovation, collective action is not just a concept; it is a transformative force that has the potential to shape our world and to think in relations. As we navigate complex problems like the COVID-19 pandemic, the climate crisis, and the poly-crisis, let us draw inspiration from the successes of collective action by reflecting on the collective flattening-the-curve moment, fostering a collective mindset that emphasizes collaboration, shared responsibility, and a determination to build a sustainable future. By building for planet, we can create a lasting impact and leave a regenerative legacy for generations to come.

CHAPTER 5: WAVES OF RAPID INNOVATION

Throughout history, it has been shown that crisis often leads to innovation. The financial crash of 2008 resulted in the widespread adoption of cloud technology as startups and corporations sought cost-effective solutions. This also led to the rise of innovation such as the sharing economy, with its applications used by new startups like Airbnb and Uber emerging. Crises also provide opportunities for entirely new ideas to take shape. For example, nuclear power and the first rockets were both outcomes of World War II. It will be not so wrong to state that the COVID pandemic was *the Sputnik moment* of our generation – when our society recognized the need to keep up with the technological and scientific advancements required.

In Peter H. Diamandis' futures forecast, the 2020s will trigger waves of exponential technological advancements stacking atop one another, eclipsing decades of breakthroughs in scale and impact, also known as the singularity. Indeed rapid innovation is happening at an unprecedented pace, and businesses must prepare to ride the waves of change or risk being left behind. With the rise of disruptive technologies like mRNA, Web 3.0, generative AI; global competition, and changing customer preferences, businesses and their founders must innovate quickly to stay relevant. However, in the age of singularity, businesses that prioritize speed over direction risk going in the wrong direction.

This chapter explores the challenges and opportunities of much-needed rapid innovation and how agile startups can navigate the waves of change by reflecting on the pandemic and beyond. Startups, by their very nature, are often at the forefront of innovation, and being equipped with the strategies and tools to navigate rapid change can give them a competitive edge. Understanding the patterns, trends, and potential pitfalls of rapid innovation allows startups and their founders to make informed decisions, adapt their business models, and pivot when necessary, maximizing their chances of success in a rapidly evolving market. Let's begin by discussing four key lessons learned from the pandemic about achieving rapid innovation.

Speed is Not Direction

Businesses that focus solely on speed risk going in the wrong direction. Companies that prioritize speed over direction may produce quick solutions to problems but may not solve the right problems. Blockbuster, Kodak, and Nokia are examples of companies that failed to balance speed and direction in achieving rapid innovation. They failed to anticipate changing customer preferences and technological advances that disrupted their industries. To achieve rapid innovation, businesses must have a clear direction and prioritize speed to stay ahead of the competition. Many companies acknowledge the importance of being fast in times of rapid change and uncertainty. According to the McKinsey survey, the primary reason for organizational changes during the pandemic was the necessity to respond swiftly to market fluctuations. This reason is cited much more frequently than other factors like cost reduction, productivity enhancement, or improved customer engagement. However if the direction is wrong, speed does not matter, in fact, it might take us to different results with some unintended negative outcomes.

That is why businesses of all sizes must define their impact vision, mission, and long-term goals. When working with impact entrepreneurs this long-term vision is often called a theory of change. This roadmap, which I frame it as an impact model, defines which activities and resources are needed to create the change needed by the stakeholders, whether they are users, customers, or beneficiaries. This clarity of purpose serves as a guiding light, ensuring that all innovation efforts are aligned with the overarching strategic objectives and the needs of stakeholders.

By establishing a clear direction, founders can focus their resources and efforts on initiatives that are most likely to drive impactful innovation, reducing the risk of wasted time, increasing their impact, and being sure that resources are used on relevant pursuits.

That is why direction is much more important than speed. Because if you're traveling in the right direction, sooner or later your destination will be reached. Which is the *point*.

Tapping into Niche Markets

By definition, an entrepreneur is a person who can turn problems into opportunities. COVID has surfaced many of the problems the modern economies inherently have. From the fragility of the supply chain to the unequal distribution of wealth we are living not only in the age of singularity but also an epoch of poly-crisis. Many solutions in the market often target where the consumers are. That is why companies develop products and services where the bulk of the consumers are. However, COVID showed us that there are people in the extremes, beyond the middle of a reversed U-shape normal distribution. In fact, just like the innovation curve, the markets do not operate on the basis of a normal distribution where the users are in the middle, but at the right end of a long tail. Remember the creators from TikTok and YouTube popularized during the lockdowns. It was a perfect example of long tail markets. The future of entertainment is in the millions of niche markets at the shallow end of the bitstream. Coined by Chris Anderson long-tail is a business strategy to sell high volumes of popular items while also selling lower volumes of thousands of less popular, or niche, items. This is the new reality of poly-crisis, a distributed market aiming to solve the problems of niche, usually their needs not catered to by the mainstream.

Moving from the creator economy of influencers that we have witnessed during the pandemic, in the age of poly-crisis we have many unmet needs due to the challenges ahead. Whether solving retail during the lockdown or retrofitting car engines by swapping them with battery-powered engines as Oxfordshire-based Electrogenic does challenge-driven solutions are solutions that are created to address specific challenges or problems. Businesses can use challenges to identify opportunities for innovation and quickly develop solutions to address them. The XPRIZE Foundation and OpenIDEO are examples of organizations that use challenge-driven solutions to drive rapid innovation. The XPRIZE Foundation is a nonprofit organization that designs and manages public competitions to encourage technological development that could benefit humanity. OpenIDEO is a platform for creative problem-solving that brings together a community of designers, thinkers, and innovators to tackle complex social issues. This is the direction we need.

Radical Collaboration Needs a Direction

Collaboration that goes beyond traditional boundaries and brings together diverse stakeholders to solve complex problems is known as radical collaboration. Radical collaboration, influenced by design thinking, is centered around the principle of learning from others and embracing diverse perspectives throughout the problem-solving, idea generation, solution development, and innovation processes. Without a clear direction, radical collaboration can become disorganized, unfocused, and fail to produce meaningful results. For instance, The Human Genome Project and the development of the Internet are examples of radical collaboration that led to rapid innovation. The Human Genome Project was an international collaboration to map the human genome, and it resulted in new treatments for genetic diseases. The development of the Internet was a collaboration between government, academia, and industry that led to the creation of a global network that transformed communication, commerce, and social interactions. To achieve rapid innovation through radical collaboration, businesses must have a clear direction, align stakeholders around a common goal, and have a process for decision-making and resource allocation. Radical collaboration needs us to upgrade our mental models from human-centered design approaches to embrace systemic thinking by utilizing relational design while building a product or service.

Firstly, having a clear direction is crucial. Businesses must establish a vision and direction that serve as guiding forces for innovation efforts. By communicating this direction to all stakeholders, businesses can ensure that everyone is working towards a common goal. This clear sense of purpose minimizes confusion and enables focused innovation.

Secondly, stakeholder alignment is essential. Radical collaboration requires the alignment of diverse stakeholders, including employees, partners, customers, and external experts. In order to understand the relations between these stakeholders, an approach called stakeholder mapping can be used.

In addition to stakeholder alignment, businesses need to establish an efficient decision-making process. This involves defining clear roles and responsibilities, empowering teams to make decisions within their areas of expertise and providing a framework for evaluating and selecting ideas and projects. Streamlining the decision-making process ensures swift progress and avoids bottlenecks that can hinder innovation. Then the question becomes how we might have efficient decision-making systems while being agile in crisis times. While typical management structures come from the industrial revolution and militaristic organizations, the pandemic proved that these modes of operation can be slow to change especially where there is pressure coming from different angles of markets. For agility systems like holacracy can work better. To start, holacracy is a management practice in the modern era. It embraces our individual humanity, autonomy, and creative problem-solving capacities. Rather than working in hierarchies people in holacratic organizations work in iteratively evolving roles, in which one person can have several roles, which is a better fit for startups working in constant change.

Furthermore, resource allocation plays a vital role in driving rapid innovation. Businesses must allocate resources effectively, including financial resources, human capital, time, and technology. By aligning resources with the identified challenges and goals, businesses can ensure that innovation initiatives receive the necessary support and can progress at an accelerated pace. Prioritizing resource allocation based on the potential impact and feasibility of projects optimizes the use of available resources.

Building a collaborative and non-hierarchical culture is also crucial for radical collaboration. Businesses should foster an environment that encourages open dialogue, knowledge sharing, and cross-functional collaboration. This can be achieved through team-building activities, creating dedicated spaces for collaboration, and providing tools and platforms that facilitate communication and idea sharing. By nurturing a culture that values collaboration, businesses can unlock the collective intelligence and creativity of their teams, driving innovation forward in the right direction.

Design Solutions That Empower People To Heal Spaceship Earth

What makes a person entrepreneurial? This is the question I've asked many young talent who want to become the founders of their own ventures. Is it the opportunity, the problem, or a need that they see in the market? As an operator and acceleration designer in the social impact ecosystem for over a decade I faced the urgency and importance of having a holistic approach to venture building and impact modeling. For founders, it is not enough to simply develop solutions to the problems we face; we must also create solutions that inspire and empower people to take action.

The key to designing solutions that empower people is to create a sense of ownership and responsibility. People need to feel that they are part of the solution and that their actions can make a real difference. This can be achieved through education, awareness-raising campaigns, and community engagement. Impact modeling is a powerful tool to understand which of our actions can actually create an intended and unintended positive or negative impact.

That is why system thinking can be a useful toolkit for a founder. The pandemic has highlighted the interconnectedness of our planet's systems. When certain factors, such as the loss of biodiversity, accumulate and reinforce each other, it can lead to widespread failures within the overall system. An example of this is the spread of zoonotic viruses, which can be a consequence of the breakdown in biodiversity. There are many reasons why founders should consider building solutions to heal the planet. For one, it is becoming increasingly clear that our current economic and social systems are not sustainable in the long term. Climate crisis, resource depletion, and other environmental challenges are putting our planet and its inhabitants at risk. By building solutions that address these challenges, founders have the opportunity to create businesses that are not only financially successful but also contribute to a more sustainable and just future.

Buckminster Fuller, an American inventor and futurist, was a strong advocate for using technology to create a more sustainable and equitable world. He believed that humanity had the potential to create a world where everyone had access to the resources they needed to thrive, and where the planet's ecosystems were protected and regenerated.

Fuller's work on sustainable design and energy-efficient architecture, as well as his advocacy for a more equitable distribution of resources, are still influential today. Many founders and entrepreneurs are inspired by his vision of a world where technology is used for the greater good, and are working to create businesses that align with this vision.

In addition to the moral imperative to design sustainable businesses, there are also practical reasons why founders should consider building solutions to heal the planet. For one, consumers are increasingly looking for products and services that align with their values around sustainability and social responsibility. By building businesses that address these concerns, founders can tap into a growing market and build a loyal customer base that believes in their mission.

Distributed Nature of Future and Web 3.0: The Next Wave of Innovation

Innovation is an ever-evolving and dynamic force that shapes the way we live and work. Just like the wind, it can change direction and adjust its path based on the environment and circumstances. Innovation requires a flexible and adaptable mind that is open to new ideas and ways of thinking. It's about constantly pushing the boundaries of what we know and understand, and continuously learning and improving.

To truly harness the power of innovation, we must cultivate a mindset that embraces change and sees challenges as opportunities for regeneration and distribution. We must be willing to experiment, take risks, and embrace new technologies and ideas that can drive positive change.

Innovation is not just about creating new products or technologies, but about fundamentally transforming the way we approach problems and find solutions. By tapping into our creative potential and continuously expanding our understanding, we can unlock the full potential of innovation and create a better world for ourselves and future generations.

The COVID-19 pandemic brought about a new era of innovation, with digital transformation at the forefront of change. The introduction of Web 3.0 technologies has been a significant development in this space, providing a new set of tools for businesses to create decentralized and more equitable systems. Web 3.0 refers to a vision of the internet that goes beyond the traditional web model, enabling decentralized and more equitable systems. It introduces a range of innovative technologies and concepts, such as blockchain, decentralized applications (DApps), smart contracts, and decentralized finance (DeFi), among others.

At its core, Web 3.0 aims to empower individuals by giving them greater control over their data, privacy, and digital identities. Unlike Web 2.0, which is characterized by centralized platforms and services that collect and monetize user data, Web 3.0 seeks to shift the power dynamics by enabling peer-to-peer interactions and removing the need for intermediaries.

One area where Web 3.0 has shown promise is hyper localization and regeneration. By leveraging blockchain technology, Web 3.0 allows for the creation of decentralized marketplaces, enabling local communities to interact and transact without relying on centralized intermediaries. This approach supports the growth of small businesses and local economies while fostering social connections and strengthening local communities. Additionally, the concept of regeneration has emerged, with Web 3.0 technology enabling the creation of circular economies that prioritize sustainability and equitable distribution of resources. The introduction of Web 3.0 has brought about exciting possibilities for innovation, and it will be exciting to see how these technologies continue to drive positive change in the post-COVID era.

Barry Lord's work on the link between human creativity and Earth's resources is particularly relevant in the context of Web 3.0 and post-COVID innovation. Lord is a renowned advocate for the integration of cultural and environmental sustainability, emphasizing the importance of recognizing the interconnectedness between human creativity and the Earth's resources.

In his research and writings, Lord highlights how the creative process and the utilization of resources are deeply intertwined. He emphasizes the need for a holistic approach that considers the environmental impact of creative endeavors, taking into account the sourcing of materials, energy consumption, and the long-term sustainability of artistic and innovative practices.

The principles put forth by Barry Lord resonate with the ethos of Web 3.0 and post-COVID innovation. Web 3.0 technologies, with their focus on decentralization, transparency, value creation, and equitable resource distribution, provide an opportunity to integrate sustainability practices into the very fabric of digital innovation. By leveraging blockchain technology, businesses and individuals can track and verify the environmental impact of their activities, ensuring responsible resource utilization and fostering a more sustainable and regenerative approach.

As the world increasingly shifts towards distributed and renewable energy sources, we are likely to see a fundamental transformation in our cultural values and artistic expressions. With the hyperlocalization of energy production and the emergence of decentralized systems, there is an opportunity to foster a distributed and regenerative future.

Web 3.0 technologies can play a crucial role in this transformation, enabling us to rethink how we organize our communities, communicate, and assign value to art. By leveraging blockchain and other decentralized technologies, we can create new systems that empower founders, creatives, and communities to participate in the creation and distribution of solutions in a more equitable and sustainable way.

In this distributed and regenerative future, the role of ventures may also evolve. They will become more decentralized, with a greater emphasis on community engagement and the creation of collaborative, interactive experiences that reflect the values and priorities of the communities they serve. For instance, a decentralized venture in the future could involve a local community coming together to create a shared urban garden space, where residents actively participate in cultivating organic produce, sharing resources, and organizing educational workshops on sustainable farming practices.

Lord's work reminds us that our cultural values and artistic expressions are deeply intertwined with our relationship to the Earth's resources. As we continue to innovate in the post-COVID era, we have an opportunity to reimagine our relationship with energy and to create a more sustainable and equitable future for all.

One promising field worth investing in and exploring is ReFi. A newly coined term with a twist on Distributed Finance (DeFi), regenerative finance (ReFi) is an emerging field that seeks to leverage financial resources for the regeneration of ecological and social systems. One example of regenerative finance is the creation of community-led investment funds, which provide capital for local projects that generate social and environmental benefits. These funds are often structured as cooperatives, allowing community members to pool their resources and make collective decisions about how to invest them.

Another example of regenerative finance as an impact hyperstructure (a structure built on top of something else) is impact investing, which aims to generate positive social and environmental outcomes alongside financial returns. Impact investors invest in companies, organizations, and funds that prioritize sustainability and social impact. These investments can support various projects, from renewable energy to regenerative agriculture.

Web 3.0 technologies have the potential to revolutionize regenerative finance by creating decentralized and transparent financial systems. Through the use of blockchain technology, Web 3.0 platforms can enable secure and transparent transactions, track the impact of investments, and facilitate peer-to-peer lending and crowdfunding.

For example, a Web 3.0 platform could enable a community to create a decentralized investment fund that is managed by its members using smart contracts. The platform could also allow for the creation of digital assets, such as tokens, that represent ownership in regenerative projects. Investors could use these tokens to support projects that align with their values and track the impact of their investments in real time.

Overall, regenerative finance represents a promising avenue for aligning financial systems with the goals of social and environmental regeneration. As Web 3.0 technologies continue to evolve, they could play a key role in enabling the creation of more equitable and sustainable financial systems.

In conclusion, the COVID-19 pandemic has taught us valuable lessons about the power of innovation in addressing complex global challenges in creating value. From the importance of agility, flat organizations and adaptability to the significance of, the pandemic has demonstrated that crisis is the time when we need to rise to the next level and work together. We have to jump over our own shadows. As Albert Einstein once said, "You can't solve a problem on the same level that it was created. You have to rise above it to the next level." This holds true for innovation and finding solutions to the world's biggest challenges. By continuing to push the boundaries of what is possible and working together, we can create a better, more resilient future for all.

CHAPTER 6: FUTURE OF WORK

The future of work is here. COVID accelerated most of the changes and like any good crisis, made it visible to the naked eye. The workforce is in the midst of a significant transformation, not only because of the change of jobs but also the change of values. The latter creates pressure to find the right talent for companies, including startups. What the COVID pandemic emphasizes is that in the information age, time matters more than space, as the labor work can be distributed as long as capital and visions are aligned. With the increased visibility of fundamentals trends, we have witnessed the popping up of terms like remote jobs, and Great Resignation. Quite Quitting and Climate Quitters. But fundamentally, most of the changes were happening as a deep wave even before the pandemic. What the pandemic did was make them more visible. The underlying cause was not only climate, or resigning to start their own business but the need for a better alignment. Alignment of talent and purpose in life. Where talent is scarce and the competition to find the right talent for your new startup, having purposeful work is more relevant than ever. In this chapter, we will delve into the strategies that how startups and their founders can employ to attract and retain top talent in this evolving landscape. Let's dive into the dynamic shifts in our work environments, the opportunities they present, and the strategies necessary to thrive in this new era of work.

The Future of Distributed Work is Here

The pandemic has accelerated the development of digital technologies including automation and artificial intelligence. Companies initially started to use them to control costs or minimize uncertainty but also the COVID-19 pandemic has highlighted the potential of distributed work, as it has become a necessity for many businesses to operate during the pandemic. Different than the remote work itself, distributed work has been made possible through the use of technology, such as video conferencing (remember the zoom fatigue after back-to-back meetings where your calendar actually managed you), collaboration tools, and cloud computing, which allow employees to work from anywhere in the world and beyond. To simply put, remote work is a discipline for the individual worker, but distributed work is a discipline for the entire organization. Before the pandemic, we knew it was possible in individual cases but only with the pandemic, we have explored the realities of the future of work through the distributed workforce.

The COVID-19 pandemic has brought about significant changes in remote work distribution. Many companies have implemented or plan to implement long-term work-from-home policies. Chris Marsh, Research Director at 451 Research, has spent the last decade investigating the full range of tools associated with workforce productivity and advising companies how to use them effectively. His research shows that shows that 75% of companies have implemented or plan to implement work-from-home policies, with 38% expecting these changes to be long-term or permanent. Such changes have significant implications for companies and employees alike. Companies must decide whether to give their employees more autonomy and confidence or increase their level of supervision. Employees should also choose employers based on how they feel and how effective they can be in a remote work environment. Organizations need to make their business processes flexible and flexible to enable distributed work. Sociocracy tools like holacracy can help founders and first-time founders. In my experience as a first-time founder, while managing a young team, setting up circles to define their work not only solved the many questions I have received which increased my productivity but also enabled a learning environment.

Furthermore, by implementing robust guidelines and expectations for distributed work, businesses can create an environment of clarity, accountability, and optimal productivity. When employees are aware of what is expected from them and have a well-defined structure to navigate, they are empowered to work effectively, efficiently, and in harmony with their remote colleagues.

Virtual Communities Led Community-Driven Ventures

As remote and distributed work becomes more prevalent, the importance of virtual communities is also increasing. These communities bring together individuals who work remotely or who are located in different geographical locations but share common interests or goals. General Partner at Ganas Ventures Lolita Taub believes that companies with community at the core will become unicorns and produce outsized returns. But what are they? According to Taub, community-driven ventures have three main pillars where the customers identify as members, members are able to create value for other members, and finally, members start the marketing and sales flywheel. These are essential for the growth of business and also the community as the community nurtures passionate members and sticky products, they have better gross margins because engaged users support others and engage in sharing product feedback, and these businesses have lower operating and sales costs from that marketing/sales flywheel.

These communities provide a platform for members to connect, share their experiences, and learn from one another. Networking within these communities can lead to new job opportunities, collaborations, and partnerships.

In addition to networking, distributed virtual communities provide opportunities for knowledge sharing. Members of these communities can share information about industry trends, best practices, and new tools and technologies. This can lead to professional development opportunities and help individuals stay up-to-date with the latest developments in their field.

Finally, distributed virtual communities also provide opportunities for social interaction. These communities can be a source of support and camaraderie for individuals who work remotely or are geographically isolated. Facilitated and curated connections can function as masterclasses where each community member can get the collective mind of others in the circle. Through such interactions, members can share their experiences, discuss common challenges, and provide emotional support to one another. As entrepreneurship can be quite a lonely journey, such communities can accelerate organizational and individual growth.

However, it is important to recognize that virtual communities can only provide as much value as the active participation and contribution of their members. To fully reap the benefits and unlock the true potential of distributed virtual communities, individuals must go beyond being passive observers and become actively engaged participants.

Nurturing Successful Communities Support Businesses

As with the social distancing and lockdowns several distributed virtual communities thrived, providing support and resources to people seek a common goal. This virtual space functioned more than a forum website of the 2000s. In fact, such communities showed the potential of building a community-driven business. A community-first venture or a community-driven company is one that puts the community first. The community is the stakeholder which is why a company exists in addition to profit making. The community does not have to be only customers or users but anyone who can benefit from what the company is doing, hence beneficiaries. What unites the community is the shared vision and mission of the venture. COVID showed us the need to belong somewhere, and some companies build their growth on the notion of such virtual communities.

One of my favourite online communities itself has a great flywheel of growth strategy. Started as a dinner event exclusive to founders On Deck, a distributed community of entrepreneurs and professionals saw significant growth during the pandemic. The community provides members with access to resources, mentorship, and networking opportunities. As remote work became more prevalent, On Deck became a valuable resource for individuals seeking to connect with other professionals and learn new skills.

Similarly, Ship30for30, a writing community that challenges members to write and ship a 300-word essay every day for 30 days, saw a surge in membership during the pandemic. The community provides members with accountability and support, helping individuals develop their writing skills and build a daily writing habit. This community showed me that writing is how we communicate, and beyond writing itself, even in the age of generative AI, writing is not for others but also for the self, it is for thinking more clearly and organized.

Both OnDeck and Ship30 were amazing learning opportunities that transformed me from a wannabe to a doer. The same goes with the altMBA, an online program that provides leadership and management training. Delivered by the marketing guru Seth Godin, the program is designed for individuals seeking to upskill or transition to a new career and provides participants with a virtual community of peers, mentors, and coaches. An ideal place to prepare ourselves for the next chapter in our lives.

These examples demonstrate the importance of distributed virtual communities in providing support, resources, and opportunities for individuals seeking to thrive in the remote work environment. By connecting with others and engaging in these communities, individuals can build new skills, develop their careers, and find a sense of belonging and support. However, they are also an example of community-driven business models that not only survived the pandemic but actually thrived due to their offer to connect with others when connection during the pandemic was scarce.

As discussed in earlier chapters, the pandemic showed us that the future is gonna be distributed and regenerative. That is why, these communities not only explore the potential of distributed future but also highlight the potential of Web 3.0 technologies. As these technologies continue to evolve, we can expect to see new and innovative ways of connecting and collaborating with others, even in remote or geographically isolated environments. The future of work will be shaped by these emerging technologies and the distributed virtual communities they enable, providing exciting opportunities for individuals and businesses alike.

Fostering Belonging and Social Connection in the Distributed and Future Work Era is Essential

Research conducted by the International Group for the Development of Indigenous Groups defines a sense of community as a group of individuals who share important aspects of their lives and maintain heterogeneous relationships. People turned to platforms like Zoom to keep in touch with friends and colleagues, Google Classroom to teach their kids, Virtual Run to keep in touch with gym buddies This growing need has led to the demand for the internet are communities that can quickly develop alternatives to traditional networks. With over 300 million users, Zoom has seen a 50% increase in daily users since the lockdown began. As we adjust to the migration of our lives online, we have seen an unprecedented level of connectivity in recent weeks. We find ourselves joining Zoom calls, joining WhatsApp groups and attending virtual events.

To address the challenge of social isolation in remote and distributed work environments, it is also crucial for companies and organizations to create opportunities for social interaction and community building. According to a study conducted by Buffer, a leading remote work company, 19% of remote workers cited loneliness as their biggest struggle with remote work (Buffer State of Remote Work Report). To combat this, virtual team-building activities, online social events, and participation in distributed virtual communities can play a vital role in fostering a sense of belonging and connection among remote workers.

One example of a company that has successfully built a sense of community among remote workers is Buffer. This social media management platform has a fully distributed team and has developed several strategies to foster a sense of belonging among employees. These strategies include virtual coffee breaks, online games, and a virtual book club.

Another example is Automattic, the company behind WordPress, which has a fully distributed workforce and has developed a culture of inclusivity and community. The company hosts virtual events, including talent shows and game nights, to foster connections and build relationships among employees. By prioritizing social connection and community building, companies can create a sense of belonging among remote workers, leading to increased job satisfaction, productivity, and retention.

In addition to company-led initiatives, founders and HR roles can also take steps to build a sense of community in remote or distributed work environments. This includes actively engaging with distributed virtual communities, participating in virtual events, and seeking out mentorship and networking opportunities.

In the ever-evolving landscape of customer engagement and product development, virtual communities have also emerged as powerful platforms for companies to connect with their customers and gather valuable feedback.

One example of a company using a virtual community to collect customer and developer feedback is Nothing, a consumer electronics company. Nothing has been using Discord, a popular chat platform, to create a community of developers and enthusiasts who are interested in their products.

By using Discord, a mobile electronics company founded by Carl Pei, Nothing has been able to engage with customers and developers in real time, gather feedback, and build a community of supporters around their brand. The company has used distributed chat applications and social media to share updates, answer questions, and solicit feedback on everything from product design to marketing strategy.

In addition to using tools like Discord, Nothing has also created a community on Reddit, where customers and developers can share feedback and ask questions. By leveraging these virtual communities, the Nothing team has been able to build a loyal fan base and create a more collaborative and transparent product development process. By leveraging online platforms like Discord and Reddit, companies can create a space for open communication and collaboration with their stakeholders, ultimately leading to better products and stronger customer relationships by tapping the potential of collective intelligence.

While the specific tools and platforms may evolve over time, the essence of virtual communities is rooted in listening and engaging with communities to create better products, services, and experiences. As the saying goes, "It used to be that people were born as part of a community and had to find their place as individuals, while now people are born as individuals and have to find their community". This shift in how we view community and individualism is reflected in the growing importance of virtual communities and the need for companies to leverage them to build stronger relationships and create more collaborative and inclusive workplaces.

Looking ahead, the rise of Web 3.0, generative AI and blockchain technology will likely bring about even more innovative ways for companies to engage with their communities and create value for their stakeholders. As the digital landscape continues to evolve, it is important for companies to stay agile and adapt to these changes, while remaining committed to building strong and meaningful relationships with their communities. I firmly believe that the future of venture building lies in the realm of online contextual communities.

The Emergence of Web 3.0 and Passion Economy

As people around the world were forced to stay at home and practice social distancing due to COVID-19, many turned to new and innovative ways to pursue their passions and make a living doing what they love. This has led to the acceleration of what is known as the "Passion Economy."

From a production and supply perspective, the Passion Economy is a new economic model in which individuals are able to monetize their passions and skills in new and innovative ways, in a way to turn individuals into microentrepreneurs. This model is driven by the emergence of new technologies, such as the internet, 5G connections, Hi-Fi content creation tools, and blockchain, which are providing new opportunities for individuals to connect with audiences and monetize their work.

One of the keyways in which COVID-19 has accelerated the

Passion Economy is through the increase in demand for creation due to high adaptation of distributed work. With more people working from home, there has been an increased demand for online content, courses, and services that cater to individuals looking to pursue their passions and develop new skills. This has led to the emergence of new online platforms, such as On Deck and altMBA, which provide opportunities for individuals to connect with like-minded individuals and pursue their passions.

In addition, the COVID-19 pandemic has also led to the emergence of new business models in the creative industries. For example, the use of direct-to-consumer platforms and the use of cryptocurrency and blockchain technology has provided new opportunities for creators to monetize their work and connect with audiences.

Direct-to-consumer platforms empower creators to showcase their work, whether it be music, art, writing, or other forms of digital content, to a global audience. By leveraging these platforms, creators can bypass traditional gatekeepers and distribution channels, gaining greater control over their artistic endeavors and establishing direct connections with their fans. This direct interaction not only fosters a sense of community but also provides an opportunity for creators to receive immediate feedback, understand their audience's preferences, and tailor their offerings accordingly.

The integration of cryptocurrency and blockchain technology further enhances the potential of these direct-to-consumer platforms. Cryptocurrencies, such as Bitcoin or Ethereum, offer secure and decentralized transactions, eliminating the need for intermediaries and reducing transaction costs. These developments led to new types of ventures and founders, such as crypto-native and AI-native genres. Through their business models these brands of founder-turned-to-creator can leverage cryptocurrencies as a means of monetizing their work, accepting direct payments from their audience without relying on traditional financial systems.

Additionally, blockchain technology provides a transparent and immutable record of transactions and interactions. In the age of eroded collective trust, this level of transparency builds trust and enhances the relationship between creators and their audiences. Audiences can verify the authenticity of limited-edition artworks, track the provenance of digital assets, and even participate in the governance of creator-driven platforms through decentralized decision-making processes.

The rise of the Passion Economy and therefore creative economy also has important implications for the future of work. As distributed work/supply and online platforms continue to grow in popularity, individuals will have more opportunities to pursue their passions and monetize their skills. This has the potential to unlock new sources of income and create a more fulfilling and meaningful life for individuals.

One notable thought leader in this space is Li Jin, who has been exploring the concept of the Passion Economy in the context of creative industries. Li Jin argues that the Passion Economy is particularly relevant in the current context, as more and more people are looking for ways to pursue their passions and make a living doing what they love. This is driven by several factors, including the rise of remote work, the increasing importance of personal branding, and the growing demand for unique and authentic experiences.

Jin's work on the Passion Economy provides a new and exciting perspective on the future of work and has important implications for the creative industries and beyond. By embracing the Passion Economy, individuals can unlock new sources of income, build stronger relationships with their audiences, and create a more fulfilling and meaningful life. In the age of unbundling as not only media but also other means of production is being distributed, the passion economy not only provides an alternative to production but also extends the ever-growing long-tail of options to cater to the needs of masses who thrive for a niche. Most creators are afraid to niche down because they want to make something for everyone, but all you need is actually one more person than yourself.

The Talent Gap is Getting Bigger

With the supply of creation getting distributed and the production systems getting unbundled, the pandemic has radically transformed the world of work, accelerating trends that were already underway and highlighting new challenges while simultaneously changing the priorities of the talent. While companies grapple with the long-term implications of distributed work, digital transformation, and changing consumer behaviors, they are also facing new phenomena like a wider talent gap and the Great Resignation.

The talent gap refers to the mismatch between the skills and qualifications that employers require in their workforce and the skills and qualifications that job seekers possess. This gap can arise due to factors such as technological advancements, demographic changes, and shifts in the labor market. The talent gap can lead to difficulties for employers in finding and retaining skilled employees, which can ultimately impact their productivity and competitiveness.

In addition to this talent gap, an ever-increasing phenomenon of The Great Resignation, also known as The Great Quitting refers to the growing number of employees who are leaving their jobs, often due to dissatisfaction with their current work situation. It is accompanied by a related trend known as "silent quitting" where employees disengage from their work and become less productive over time.

Another related emerging trend is what some are calling "climate quitting." As the urgency of the climate crisis becomes more apparent, employees are beginning to seek out employers who share their commitment to sustainability and environmental stewardship. In fact, as KPMG reports that one in three 18–24-year-olds have rejected a job offer based on ESG record. This trend is particularly pronounced among younger workers, who are more likely to prioritize purpose and meaning in their careers.

The urgency of transitioning our society to a green economy in response to the climate crisis was underscored in LinkedIn's 2022 Global Green Skills Report, highlighting the imperative of reimagining the future of work. The share of green talent in the workforce increased from 9.6% in 2015, to 13.3% so far in 2022 (a growth rate of 38.5%). In the past year, ~10% of job postings requiring skills have explicitly required at least one green skill. Workers are increasingly skilling in green and transitioning into green and greening jobs, driving positive net transitions into these jobs.

In this rapidly changing landscape, companies and their founders will need to adapt quickly in order to attract and retain top talent. However, simply offering higher salaries and better benefits will not be enough to win over today's job seekers. Employees are increasingly looking for a sense of purpose and meaning in their work. Companies that prioritize social and environmental responsibility and align their mission and values with those of their employees gain a significant competitive advantage in the ongoing battle for top talent.

Having a Purpose is the Only Way to Attract Sustainable Talent

With all these meta trends having a clear purpose is becoming increasingly important in the business world, not only for attracting customers but also for attracting sustainable talent that doesn't quit. In today's competitive job market, talented professionals are looking for more than just a paycheck; they want to work for companies that align with their values and provide opportunities to make a positive impact on the world.

Purpose-driven companies that prioritize purpose and social responsibility are more likely to attract and retain top talent, as employees feel a sense of fulfillment and motivation from working towards a meaningful goal. In fact, a recent survey found that 73% of employees want their job to be meaningful, and 58% would take a pay cut to work for a company with a mission they believe in.

On the other hand, companies that lack a clear purpose or social responsibility may struggle to attract and retain talented employees, as they may be seen as outdated or out of touch with the needs and values of today's workforce. This is especially true for younger generations such as Millennials and Gen Z, who prioritize purpose and sustainability in their career choices.

In the context of climate change, having a purpose-driven approach is more important than ever. As the world grapples with the urgent need to address climate change, companies that prioritize sustainability and carbon neutrality are more likely to attract the best talent in fields such as renewable energy, sustainable transportation, and circular economy.

Moreover, having a clear purpose and commitment to sustainability can also help companies address the growing issue of "climate quitting" and "silent quitting". Employees who feel that their work is not aligned with their values or that their employer is not doing enough to address climate change may leave their job, either openly or silently, leading to talent shortages and productivity losses.

Therefore, startups that want to attract and retain sustainable talent must prioritize purpose, sustainability, and regenerative practices in their operations, products, and culture. This requires a deep understanding of the values and expectations of today's workforce, as well as a willingness to make long-term investments in sustainability and social responsibility. By doing so, startups can not only attract the best talent but also make a positive impact on the world and contribute to the transition toward a more sustainable future.

While distributed work and digitalization have been at the forefront of discussions on the future of work, it is the underlying movement towards purposeful work that emerges as the true linchpin in attracting and retaining top talent critical for business success. Companies must adopt a purpose-driven approach and actively create positive social or environmental impact to resonate with the values of younger consumers and potential employees. Founders and businesses that fail to recognize this paradigm shift would hinder their ability to attract and retain the best talent as well as become overshadowed in a world that increasingly prioritizes sustainability and social impact. In essence, purposeful work is no longer a mere luxury for startups or companies; it has become the indispensable pathway to relevance and competitiveness in a post-normal business landscape.

CHAPTER 7: THE BEGINNING OF THE END

Change is an inherent part of the entrepreneurial journey and the pursuit of innovation. Founders and innovators constantly face the need to adapt and evolve, particularly in the aftermath of disruptive events such as the global pandemic. However, it is crucial to approach change with caution, avoiding the trap of *hyperdiscounting* the future and short-sighted decision-making. In this chapter, we will delve into the strategies and frameworks that can aid organizations in effectively navigating the complexities of change.

While 2020 was all about the disease and the unknown, 2021 was more about solutions and vaccination efforts. The rollout of COVID-19 vaccines has been a significant turning point in the fight against the virus. As more and more people receive their vaccinations, the number of new cases, hospitalizations, and deaths have begun to decline. This has allowed many countries to ease restrictions and return to a more normal way of life.

However, the story of the vaccine rollout has been one of stark inequalities. While some countries have been able to quickly and efficiently distribute vaccines to their populations, others have faced significant obstacles and delays. This has led to disparities in access to vaccines and unequal protection against the virus.

One of the main challenges in the vaccine rollout has been the limited availability of doses. Many countries have struggled to secure enough vaccines to meet the demand of their populations, and some have resorted to prioritizing certain groups or regions over others. This has resulted in unequal access to vaccines, with essential workers, vulnerable populations, and marginalized communities often being left behind.

Another challenge has been the unequal distribution of resources and infrastructure to support the vaccine rollout. Developed countries with well-established health systems have been better equipped to handle the logistics of vaccine distribution, while poorer countries have faced significant hurdles in getting vaccines to their populations.

Despite these inequalities, the vaccination effort represents a significant step forward in the fight against COVID-19. As more and more people receive their vaccines, the world will continue to move closer to herd immunity and the end of this pandemic.

However, it is important to acknowledge and address the inequalities that have arisen in the vaccine rollout, so that everyone has the opportunity to be protected from the virus. While vaccinations deserve a chapter of their own in the next pages, in this chapter, we will focus on the innate human tendency to seek hope in liminal moments. Liminal moments refer to those transitional periods when individuals and organizations are at the threshold of change. During such moments, the human mind often seeks solace in the anticipation of positive outcomes, leading to a tendency to prematurely frame situations and their consequences.

Understanding this psychological inclination is crucial for founders and entrepreneurs who wish to navigate change effectively. By approaching change management with this type of measured and thoughtful mindset, organizations can avoid undue optimism or pessimism and make decisions that align with the reality of the situation.

Furthermore, in this chapter, we will delve into another compelling question: How can we develop the foresight and awareness necessary to identify the penultimate moments of upcoming crises? We will explore the lessons learned from the vaccination efforts and apply them to the broader context of change management.

While the vaccination campaigns have undoubtedly offered hope and served as a crucial milestone in addressing the immediate crisis, they also provide valuable insights into the importance of preparedness and early detection. As we reflect on the successes and challenges encountered during the vaccination rollout, we can glean lessons about how to anticipate and respond to future crises.

Change Management in Liminal and Pivotal Moments

Change management is a critical process that helps organizations navigate transitions and adapt to new circumstances effectively. However, it is during the liminal and pivotal moments that change management becomes particularly crucial. In these moments, the organization faces significant challenges, and its future is uncertain. It is essential to have a change management strategy that can help guide the organization through these uncertain times successfully. One such model that has gained popularity in recent years is William Bridges' Change Model.

This model is based on the premise that people go through three stages during a transition: ending, neutral zone, and a new beginning. The ending stage involves letting go of the old ways of doing things, while the neutral zone is a time of uncertainty and exploration. Finally, the new beginning stage involves embracing the new reality and moving forward. Bridges' model emphasizes the psychological aspects of change, and it is essential for organizations to understand the emotional journey that people go through during a transition. By understanding these stages and providing support to individuals during each stage, organizations can manage change effectively and reduce others' resistance to change.

The Cynefin framework is another concept that is often used in change management. Developed by Dave Snowden, the Cynefin framework helps organizations understand the complexity of their situation and determine the best approach to navigate it. In addition to that, this popular framework can be applied to repurpose resources and adapt to the new reality. The framework categorizes situations into five domains: simple, complicated, complex, chaotic, and disorder. Let's explore each domain in more detail and how organizations can use it to innovate for repurpose.

Simple: This domain refers to problems that have a clear cause-and-effect relationship. The solution is obvious and can be implemented quickly. In the context of the COVID-19 pandemic, simple problems may include implementing social distancing measures, providing hand sanitizers, and wearing masks. Organizations must quickly identify and implement solutions to ensure the safety of their employees and customers.

Complicated: This domain refers to problems that require expertise and analysis to solve. The solution is not obvious and requires input from subject matter experts. In the context of the COVID-19 pandemic, complicated problems included developing a vaccine, designing effective testing protocols, and managing supply chains. Organizations must engage subject matter experts to analyze the problem and provide a solution that addresses the specific challenges posed by the pandemic.

Complex: This domain refers to problems that are unpredictable and require experimentation to find a solution. The solution emerges from trial and error rather than expertise. In the context of the COVID-19 pandemic, complex problems may include implementing remote working policies, adjusting to changing customer behaviors, and designing new product offerings. Founders must always be willing to experiment and adapt their approach based on the feedback they receive.

Chaotic: This domain refers to problems that require immediate action to restore order. The situation is often unpredictable, and the solution requires a rapid response. In the context of the COVID-19 pandemic, chaotic problems may include responding to a sudden surge in cases, managing a shortage of medical supplies, and ensuring the safety of employees in high-risk areas. Organizations must act quickly to restore order and implement measures to mitigate the impact of the crisis.

Disorder: This domain refers to problems that are unclear and do not fit into any of the other domains. The solution requires a shift in perspective and an understanding of the underlying causes. In the context of the COVID-19 pandemic, disorder problems may include understanding the long-term impact of the crisis, identifying emerging opportunities, and developing a strategy for the future. Organizations must take a step back and analyze the situation to develop a comprehensive plan that addresses the underlying causes of the problem.

Cynefin Framework can be a valuable guide to help organizations innovate for repurpose during times of crisis, to reorient themselves to the new normal. By categorizing problems into the five domains, organizations, their founders, and especially startups can better understand the nature of the challenges and develop solutions that are tailored to the specific context or upcoming scenario. By embracing Cynefin Framework, ventures can emerge stronger from the crisis and position themselves for long-term success.

Back to *Normal* is Impossible

The idea of "back to normal" implies returning to a pre-crisis state, but in reality, it is often difficult or impossible to go back entirely to the way things were before. COVID-19 has created a new normal, and the world will be different in many ways post-pandemic. Rather than striving for a return to the past, it is essential for startups and innovators to consider how they can adapt to the new reality and create a better future.

Here are some suggestions for startups and innovators on how to approach the post-COVID period:

- *Embrace the new reality:* The pandemic has created a new world, which means there are new opportunities to explore. For example, the pandemic has accelerated the shift to digital, creating new opportunities for startups that provide digital solutions. Instead of resisting change, embrace it, and find new ways to add value and connect.

- *Be flexible:* Flexibility is key during times of uncertainty. Startups should be ready to pivot quickly if necessary and adjust their business models to meet changing market demands.

- *Build resilience:* The pandemic has shown how quickly things can change. Startups should focus on building resilience by diversifying their revenue streams, developing contingency plans, and investing in their team's mental health and well-being.

- *Collaborate:* The pandemic has brought people and organizations together to solve complex problems. Startups should seek out partnerships and collaborations to address the challenges created by COVID-19. For example, many startups have collaborated with healthcare providers to develop new technologies that help to combat the virus.

- *Prioritize health and safety:* COVID-19 has highlighted the importance of health and safety. Startups should prioritize the health and safety of their employees, customers, and communities. For example, some startups have implemented new safety protocols, such as contactless delivery or remote work policies, to help prevent the spread of the virus.

Ultimately, rather than striving for a return to the past, startups and innovators can embrace the new normal and focus on building a better future.

Balancing Short-Term Needs with Long-Term Vision Amidst Premature Naming

While sensemaking is a skill to be embraced, one pitfall that organizations may face during times of crisis, such as the COVID-19 pandemic, is naming things prematurely. This emerged during the pandemic when we saw the premature establishment of a post-COVID narrative in early 2021, despite the world still being in the inter-COVID period, rather than the envisioned post-pandemic era. One fundamental cause of this is hyperdiscounting, which is the tendency to place greater value on immediate rewards rather than future rewards. This tendency can lead to short-term thinking and decision-making. In the context of the pandemic, hyperdiscounting manifested as organizations solely focusing on surviving the current crisis and not adequately preparing for the post-pandemic future, or, as we stated earlier, the new normal.

In some cases, organizations may have framed their post-COVID strategy too early, while still in the midst of the pandemic. This premature framing of the post-pandemic future can lead to decisions based on incomplete or inaccurate information, which can have negative consequences in the long run. It is essential to strike a balance between managing the immediate crisis and planning for the future, using a thoughtful and deliberate approach.

The William Bridges Change Model and the Cynefin framework can help organizations avoid the pitfall of hyperdiscounting the future. By focusing on the psychological aspects of change and understanding the complexity of the situation, organizations can take a more holistic approach to change management. The Bridges model emphasizes the importance of recognizing the emotional journey of individuals during a transition, including the uncertainty and exploration of the neutral zone. The Cynefin framework helps organizations understand the complexity of their situation and determine the best approach to navigate it, avoiding oversimplified solutions that do not adequately address the situation's nuances.

For founders and innovators, the recognition of the potential pitfall of hyperdiscounting the future is crucial in navigating change. It is imperative to adopt a deliberate approach to change management, one that strikes a delicate balance between addressing immediate needs and engaging in comprehensive long-term planning. While the end of the pandemic may be in sight, its profound impacts will reverberate long after its conclusion, underscoring the significance of forward-thinking strategies.

In the pursuit of effective change management, the utilization of frameworks such as the Bridges model and the Cynefin framework provides invaluable guidance. These frameworks offer a multidimensional lens through which organizations can comprehend the complexities inherent in the process of change. By embracing these tools, organizations can circumvent the dangers of oversimplification and short-sighted thinking, paving the way for robust and adaptive transformations.

CHAPTER 8: A CONTINENTAL SHIFT

As the global economy continues to evolve, the importance of emerging markets is becoming increasingly apparent. The rise of the Asian century, the potential for African economies to drive global growth, and the unique challenges and opportunities facing entrepreneurs in emerging markets make it imperative for entrepreneurs to consider the continent shift. In this chapter, we will explore the implications of this shift and discuss strategies for entrepreneurs looking to take advantage of this new era of opportunity.

The arrival of the Asian Century was coined by Deng Xiaoping and later popularized by the author Parag Khanna. "Asian Century" is a term that refers to the idea that the 21st century will be dominated by Asia as a center of economic, cultural, and political power. This concept is based on the rapid economic growth and development that has taken place in many Asian countries in recent decades, including China, India, and Southeast Asia. The economic growth of China and India, among other Asian countries, has been unprecedented in recent decades. These countries have increasingly become dominant players in the global economy, with China currently the world's second-largest economy, and India the fifth. The potential for entrepreneurship in these countries is vast, particularly in the technology and innovation sectors. There is also an abundance of talent, with a growing number of highly skilled workers, and the digital infrastructure is expanding rapidly, creating new opportunities for entrepreneurs to develop innovative products and services.

The role of government policies and investments in fostering entrepreneurship in Asia is also significant. Governments have implemented various policies and initiatives to promote entrepreneurship, including tax incentives, financial support, and business incubation programs. As a result, the number of entrepreneurs and startups has grown rapidly, and Asia has become a hub for innovation and entrepreneurship.

Case studies of successful Asian entrepreneurs and their strategies for growth can provide valuable insights for entrepreneurs looking to take advantage of the opportunities presented by the Asian century. For example, Jack Ma, the founder of Alibaba, built his empire by identifying an opportunity in e-commerce and leveraging China's unique characteristics, such as a large and growing middle class, to scale his business rapidly. Similarly, Lei Jun, the founder of Xiaomi, used a unique business model to enter the highly competitive smartphone market and became one of the largest smartphone manufacturers in the world.

Finding the Next Wave with African Opportunity

It is almost clear that somehow the African continent evaded the pandemic. "The case-fatality ratio (CFR) for COVID-19 in Africa is lower than the global CFR suggesting the outcomes have been less severe among African populations," noted a recent continental study by Partnership for Evidence-based Response to COVID-19 (PERC). While there are many underlying reasons for that one striking figure, one reason looking into is the demographics. Only 3% of the population is aged over 65 years," said Dr. Matshidiso Moeti, the WHO Africa head, which is much lower than the other continents. Also, with the population increase by 2025, there will be 100 African cities with more than one million inhabitants. With this rate of urbanization, Africa is a huge emerging market that presents a wealth of opportunity for entrepreneurs as the middle class is expanding, providing a growing market for goods and services. Moreover, African economies have been growing at an average rate of 4% per year, making it one of the fastest-growing regions in the world. In fact, Africa's 1.1 billion citizens will likely double in number by 2050, and more than 80% of that increase will occur in cities, especially slums.

That is why entrepreneurship and regenerative growth in Africa can be beneficial in many sectors. African nations have long been using high-yielding, resilient, and adaptive practices in soil, cropping, and integrated systems. Thus, it is important to acknowledge and enhance the existing practices instead of introducing new ones. This would require supporting their adoption and scaling to ensure their widespread use. Also, the digitalization and adaptation of innovation as a response to the COVID-19 crisis builds momentum for Africa's digital transformation to overcome the pandemic and create more productive jobs, according to the OECD's 2021 edition of *Africa's Development Dynamics*.

However, there are unique challenges and opportunities. While the continent has seen significant economic growth in recent years, many countries still face significant infrastructure and development challenges. However, these challenges also present opportunities for entrepreneurs to develop innovative solutions to address these issues.

With the mindset of enterprise as a service, founders can help societies to thrive. Governments have implemented various policies and initiatives to promote entrepreneurship, such as tax incentives, access to finance, and business incubation programs. Moreover, the African Union launched Agenda 2063, which is a

50-year development plan to transform Africa into a prosperous and peaceful continent, with entrepreneurship being a critical pillar of the plan.

Case studies of successful African entrepreneurs and their strategies for growth can provide valuable insights for entrepreneurs looking to take advantage of the opportunities presented by the African opportunity. For example, Strive Masiyiwa, the founder of Econet Wireless, built his empire by identifying an opportunity in mobile telecommunications in Zimbabwe and then expanding across the continent. Similarly, Ashish Thakkar, the founder of Mara Group, has built a diversified conglomerate of businesses across Africa, leveraging his extensive networks and knowledge of local markets to create successful ventures. With the planet in mind, there is a once-in-a-lifetime opportunity to make this growth green, inclusive, and regenerative.

Expanding Globally as a Startup

Startups tend to focus on their home markets in the early stages, but it's important for them to think globally. By doing so, they can broaden their customer base, gain exposure to new ideas, identify potential opportunities and partnerships, and mitigate risks. In today's interconnected world, embracing the global marketplace is crucial for startup success.

Expanding into emerging markets presents a unique set of

opportunities and challenges for entrepreneurs. On the one hand, these markets represent vast and untapped potential for growth, and entrepreneurs who can identify opportunities and develop products and services to meet the needs of these markets can reap significant rewards. On the other hand, these markets can also be complex and difficult to navigate, with unique cultural, legal, and political considerations that must be taken into account.

To expand globally, entrepreneurs must develop a deep understanding of the target market, including its culture, business environment, and regulatory landscape. This may require partnering with local entrepreneurs and experts who have deep market knowledge and can help guide the entrepreneur through the local nuances. For such global exploration, local networks and communities can give several leverages to gain a foothold in the local markets. This is called soft-landing partners.

In addition to local soft-landing partners, expanding globally requires a strategic approach to business development. Entrepreneurs must carefully consider their product offerings, pricing, and marketing strategies to ensure they resonate with the local market. This may require adapting the product or service to meet the specific needs of the local market, as well as investing in targeted marketing campaigns that are tailored to the local culture and language.

Finally, entrepreneurs must also consider the legal and regulatory environment of the target market. This may include navigating complex tax laws, securing necessary permits and licenses, and complying with local regulations. Entrepreneurs who can successfully navigate these challenges can unlock significant growth opportunities in emerging markets and position their businesses for long-term success.

Here are some tips for startups that are thinking globally:

- Research and analyze global market trends and customer needs to identify potential opportunities.
- Consider the cultural and regulatory differences of target markets and adapt the products or services accordingly.[8]
- Use communities to identify local soft-landing partners to navigate the unknowns.
- Build a diverse team with global perspectives and experiences to help navigate different markets and cultural nuances.
- Establish strategic partnerships and networks with local companies and industry experts to gain insights, access to distribution channels, and enable a soft landing.
- Leverage technology and digital platforms to reach customers and operate remotely in different markets.

---

[8] Thinking in Circles and the concept of face or mianzi (面子) is a good example of how linear and circular thinking is framed in this article https://randomwire.com/thinking-in-circles/

- Identify the stakeholders and map the journey of each and every main stakeholder group
- Continuously test and iterate (and validate) the product or service based on feedback and market demand, and build in public to get feedback from the community.
- Stay agile and adaptable to pivot the business strategy based on market trends and customer/stakeholder feedback.

By following these tips, startups can successfully navigate the global marketplace and expand their business on a global scale while also building their own global community while the markets are shifting to the East. Many founders find it difficult to compete in some western economies where the legislations are tight in some industries like healthcare or legal tech. Also Europe is lagging behind in the digitalization. Emerging Asian and African economies are more dynamic and risk-prone to test new tools and products. These factors are praised by the entrepreneurs and innovators. Targeting such expansion or even picking these markets for homebase from day one can be quite beneficial for early founders.

That is why this continental shift represents a significant opportunity for entrepreneurs to expand into emerging markets and take advantage of the unique opportunities presented by these rapidly growing economies while designing regenerative and inclusive practices. By developing a deep understanding of the target market, partnering with local entrepreneurs and experts, and taking a strategic approach to business development, entrepreneurs can unlock significant growth opportunities and position their businesses for long-term success. As we continue to navigate the COVID-19 pandemic and its economic implications, the importance of the continental shift and its implications for entrepreneurship in emerging markets will only continue to grow.

CHAPTER 9: FACING OUR SHADOWS: MULTIVERSE OF INEQUALITIES

As with any real crisis, the pandemic has undeniably put our resilience to the test, revealing profound vulnerabilities within both our physical well-being and societal structures. As we continue to grapple with the lasting repercussions of this global crisis, it becomes crucial to reflect on the valuable lessons we can learn and contemplate the possibilities that lie ahead in the greater systems that we live in.

By envisioning diverse and plausible scenarios, we can glean invaluable insights into the choices and actions that have the potential to shape the world we aspire to inhabit. Through this process, we can proactively contribute to the creation of a future that is more just, inclusive, and sustainable by leaving no one behind. This concept of leaving no one behind became the main promise of the 2030 Agenda for Sustainable Development. Unlike Millenium Development Goals, the 2030 Agenda was a result of an extensive consultation to map the stakeholders in many diverse populations. In the age of generative artificial intelligence, we have witnessed the importance of collective intelligence to map the multi-dimension of poverty as it was quite visible that A person who is poor can suffer from multiple disadvantages at the same time. With the concept of polycrisis, such vulnerabilities can trigger a chain reaction in the ecosystem we operate. We'll go into ways to sense make the social fabric and the importance of self-reflection later on in this chapter.

As we engage in this forward-thinking exercise, it is equally vital to look backward and examine the blind spots and deficiencies that the pandemic has laid bare. By critically assessing our past experiences, we can identify the areas where our responses were inadequate and recognize the shortcomings that demand our attention. This retrospective analysis serves as a crucial foundation for the necessary course corrections required to forge a more equitable future.

By combining these two approaches – forward-looking speculation and reflective analysis – we aim to equip ourselves with the knowledge and insights needed to navigate the complexities of crises and to actively shape a future that holds promise for all. In this context, the pandemic multiverse is a thought-provoking concept. This combo of speculative questioning enables us to consider what might have happened if things had gone differently, if we had made different choices and taken different actions. By exploring these alternative universes, we can gain a deeper understanding of the impact of our decisions, and the potential paths that lie ahead.

In the first universe, action against the virus was slow and inadequate, and the impact of the pandemic was devastating. But in the second universe, action was agile and effective with collective action, and the impact was much less severe. The difference between these two universes underscores the importance of quick, decisive, and collective action in the face of a crisis.

For founders, this multiverse of the pandemic offers a valuable lesson. When faced with a crisis whether at a venture level or a global level, it is essential to act quickly and decisively with information. The information is already available; however, it needs to be analyzed by gathering input from your suppliers, team members, and stakeholders to determine its significance for each of them. This approach is called stakeholder mapping. This means being agile, adaptable, and willing to make tough decisions when necessary. It also means recognizing and addressing inequalities and vulnerabilities that may make certain communities more vulnerable to the effects of the crisis.

The COVID-19 pandemic has laid bare the deep inequalities that exist in societies around the world. The impacts of the virus have not been evenly distributed, with marginalized communities and individuals bearing the brunt of the economic, health, and social consequences. In fact, the wealth of the world's 10 richest men alone has doubled, rising at a rate of $15,000 per second. But COVID-19 has left 99 percent of humanity worse off. The statistics presented in Oxfam's recent report titled "Inequality Kills" are staggering. To illustrate, the wealth of billionaires has surged during the pandemic at a higher rate than the cumulative increase of the past 14 years. Notably, renowned institutions such as the IMF, World Bank, Crédit Suisse, and World Economic Forum (WEF) all forecast a significant surge in inequality within countries. In the alternative multiverse, societies have responded to the pandemic quickly and with a focus on equality and planet-centric solutions. Instead of a slow action of flattening the curve, with a quick response they have crushed it with short-term tough measures as they understand the gravity of the challenge with better information. In addition, they have adopted measures such as universal healthcare, income support, and regenerative economic policies. These societies have been able to contain the spread of the virus, lower mortality rates, and create a more resilient society with regenerative practices.

This society prioritized collective well-being and has adopted a planet-centric approach that recognized the importance of protecting the environment and ensuring a regenerative future.

They have invested in renewable energy, green transportation, and sustainable agriculture and see planetary health as an important part of having a lesser crisis. These measures not only benefit the environment but also create purposeful jobs and harmony for the planet. Considering what Philip Lymbery said about that we have only 60 harvests left in our topsoil, such practices need to be mainstreamed by the new ventures.

No matter how dark our future looks, we are in a pivotal time to reverse the course of planetary destruction induced by modern economic systems. That is why reflecting on the pandemic and our economic system can help us to see what needs to be done. Let's get into four more important lessons from the pandemic and how we, as founders, can apply what we know now. We will explore the interconnected themes of economic inequality, societal transformation, and sustainable enterprise, aiming to unravel the threads that will weave together the fabric of a more sustainable future for all.

We Have Two Economies

The pandemic also showed us that we have two economies, one for the riches and the other for the poor. The middle class is merely a transition, a void, in this case. In this duality, racial or social inequalities make crises especially vulnerable for socioeconomically disadvantaged people. Low-prestige jobs, like frontline healthcare workers and sanitation workers, involve significant physical risks. Throughout the pandemic, these individuals faced heightened exposure to hazards and health threats, highlighting the disparities in risk and reward within our society. COVID-19 also has exposed a harsh truth about our society: the rich are getting richer while the poor are struggling to survive. While some people have become billionaires during this time, others have lost their livelihoods, homes, and even their lives.

It's disturbing to see how the pandemic has widened the gap between the haves and have-nots. The global lockdowns have caused a severe economic recession that has hit the most vulnerable populations the hardest. Millions of people have lost their jobs, and many businesses have closed down permanently.

It's important to recognize that this is not just a function of capitalism, but rather a reflection of the ways in which our economy is structured, valuing profit over impact and short-term gains over long-term sustainability. The pandemic has accelerated the shift toward a digital economy, and this has benefited those who have been able to capitalize on this trend. At the same time, it has hit those in the service sector and other industries hard. However, it's important to recognize that capitalism has also played a role in driving innovation and growth and that it has created many jobs and opportunities for people around the world. The challenge we face is to find ways to ensure that the benefits of this system are shared more equitably and that we work towards a more inclusive and sustainable future.

As founders, it is crucial for us to recognize the potential for positive change that the pandemic has brought to light. We should seize this opportunity, and new normal, to tackle underlying issues and foster a more just and equitable society. A promising approach gaining momentum in recent years is the "bottom of the pyramid" economy, which emphasizes the creation of affordable and accessible products and services for individuals with the lowest incomes.

By adopting this approach, we can not only address poverty and inequality but also unlock new markets and opportunities for businesses that are willing to think innovatively and collaborate closely with local communities. This mindset enables us to build a more resilient and sustainable economy that benefits everyone.

The concept of the bottom-of-the-pyramid approach is further reinforced when we consider the pandemic multiverse. In a scenario where the pandemic's impact was less severe, it became evident that reaching out to the most vulnerable and underserved individuals at the bottom of the pyramid is of utmost importance.

For founders, this presents an exceptional business opportunity with a significant social impact. By focusing on the needs of those at the bottom of the pyramid and developing products and services that address their unique challenges and vulnerabilities, we can make a meaningful difference in the world while also building a profitable and sustainable business.

The pandemic has served as a reminder of the interconnectedness of our world and the interdependence of our well-being. By embracing a bottom-of-the-pyramid approach, founders have the power to contribute to the creation of a more equitable and resilient world. In this world, everyone will have access to the necessary resources and support to thrive and succeed. That is why in the future any business that won't have any impact case would not have a business case.

Societal Structures are Fluid, Not Frozen

As a response to inequalities and shareholder capitalism, we have witnessed a reaction to the narrative of going back to normal. The sentiment over the old normal was greeted with phrases like, "We won't get back to normal because normal was the problem." But what *is* the next normal and how can we collectively create an even better alternative? As Otto Scharmer beautifully captures in his own pandemic reflections, in the Anthropocene, humans are the main source of problems that we face. This is because our ways of thinking and acting are often outdated and no longer effective. In fact, the environment we're in often changes faster than our own brains can. However, we do have the ability to reimagine and reshape these patterns and our habits, which is where the COVID pandemic can teach us an important lesson.

The pandemic has shown us that we as humans have the power to reshape our own operating systems. We have the ability to change our societal structures, which are not set in stone, but are rather fluid and capable of evolving over time. This is a unique capability that sets humans apart from other species on Earth. It is important to recognize that the laws that govern human behavior are not fixed like the laws of nature. Instead, they can change based on the awareness and consciousness of individuals. This means that social structures are not frozen but can evolve and change as our consciousness evolves.

By applying this principle of social plasticity to the collective, we can see that we have the power to change our systems as a whole. The pandemic has shown us that we are capable of adapting and changing our behaviors to find solutions. This has led to significant shifts in societal structures, such as increased public investment in combating climate change and a commitment to net zero emissions by 2050. The lesson for founders from the COVID pandemic is that they have the power to adapt and change their businesses, just like societal structures. By recognizing that the laws that govern business behavior can change based on consciousness, founders can change their patterns of thinking and find solutions to challenges. This has led to significant shifts in the business landscape, and successful businesses are those that are willing to adapt and change their strategies.

It is time to build for *purpose and the planet.*

Building for Planet Requires an Upgrade of Our Systems

As our economy continues to grow, we are inevitably approaching a point where the planet can no longer keep up with our demand for resources. This has been a long wake-up call that forces us to redefine what prosperity truly means and how we can create an economy that cares for both people and the planet. This requires a shift in the way we think about enterprises - from shareholder capitalism to stakeholder capitalism while updating our operating system.

Under shareholder capitalism, the primary focus is on maximizing profits for shareholders, often at the expense of other stakeholders such as employees, customers, and the environment. This approach has contributed to the current state of inequality and environmental degradation. However, under stakeholder capitalism, businesses prioritize the needs of all stakeholders, not just shareholders. This includes investing in their employees, supporting their communities, and minimizing their impact on the environment.

To successfully transition to stakeholder capitalism, we must think of enterprise as a service to the future and the planet. We must consider how to recover and where to allocate our resources, all while protecting our climate and our people. We need to prioritize care and recognize that enterprise can be a powerful tool for positive change.

At its core, stakeholder capitalism is about recognizing that businesses exist to serve society, not just to maximize profits for a select few. By prioritizing the needs of all stakeholders, we can create an economy that works for everyone and protects the planet for future generations.

We Must Build Companies with a 100-Year Mindset

These lessons have underscored the pressing need to build societies that are resilient and sustainable, placing the health and well-being of all citizens at the forefront.

Stakeholder capitalism emerges as a compelling paradigm, where enterprises shift their focus beyond maximizing shareholder profits to embrace the creation of social and environmental value. By prioritizing the needs of all stakeholders - encompassing employees, customers, and the environment - businesses can actively contribute to the holistic well-being of society. This approach not only promotes greater equity but also fosters sustainability by recognizing the interconnectedness between economic prosperity, social harmony, and environmental stewardship.

Simultaneously, the bottom-of-the-pyramid approach offers a potent framework for addressing inequality and fostering a more equitable society. By directing attention to the needs of the world's poorest communities, businesses can create significant business and social impact. This inclusive approach not only bridges the gap between the haves and have-nots but also generates opportunities for growth, innovation, and collaboration, thereby contributing to a more sustainable future.

However, to truly embrace a sustainable mindset, companies, and their founders must transcend short-term thinking and adopt a long-term perspective. By cultivating a 100-year mindset, businesses can shift their focus from immediate gains to enduring impact, recognizing that their actions today reverberate across generations. This mindset prompts a recalibration of strategies and decision-making processes, encompassing the consideration of environmental conservation, social justice, and intergenerational equity.

The imperative to build companies with a 100-year mindset is an invitation to envision an enduring legacy, where enterprise serves as a force for positive change, capable of transcending the limitations of time and individual interests. It challenges entrepreneurs and leaders to integrate regeneration as a core value. By doing so, businesses can be catalysts for transformation, empowering societies to thrive in harmony with the planet and creating a future that is characterized by shared prosperity, dignity, and ecological balance.

CHAPTER 10: CHIPS AND CHAINS: FRAGILITY OF SUPPLY CHAIN SYSTENS

As the vaccinations rolled out in mass, the health toll of the pandemic which was the initial great wave of the impact started to ease out. However with the tidal wave passing over the rough 2020 and 2021, it was evident that the economic toll would leave marks in the way we do business which would require ventures to pivot.

Even from the early days of it the pandemic has brought unprecedented global disruptions to supply chains, exposing the fragilities of the complex networks that underpin the global economy. Panic buying at the onset of the pandemic was an indication of the innate human response to threats and the importance of supply security. As borders closed and air travel ceased, logistics systems ground to a halt, severely affecting manufacturing industries and leading to shortages of goods such as semiconductors, wheat, medicine and vegetable oil. The crisis demonstrated the impossibility of creating a 100% resilient supply chain, as well as the urgent need for companies to adopt reverse logistics and sustainable practices. COVID-19 has not only brought attention to the vulnerabilities of global supply chains controlled by major corporations, but it has also served as a catalyst for civil society activists advocating for the establishment of resilient, locally rooted value chains, which I believe will fundamentally change how we build and procure stuff. That is why emerging trends like *hyperlocalization* and DIY culture should be examined further as they have gained prominence as strategies to enhance supply chain stability. The crisis also highlighted the importance of collaborative efforts among industry players, governments, and society to create more sustainable, regenerative and resilient supply chains for the future. Looking back into the pandemic, let's explore the lessons learned and the ways in which founders can apply these lessons to gain a competitive advantage and be equipped to handle potential crises in the future.

In the early days of the pandemic, we observed a fascinating display of one of our species' ancient defense mechanisms. As natural hoarders, people began stockpiling essential food items, sanitary tools, and non-perishables. Initially, panic buying appeared illogical when attempting to mitigate supply risks. However, in retrospect, it is intriguing to witness how the collective wisdom of the crowds played out favorably. The closure of ports and transportation networks in China had a profound impact on factory lockdowns, resulting in a scarcity of both staff and goods, further exacerbating the polycrisis.

In the first days of the pandemic, we closely watched the maps turn red with each day showing the spread of the virus. China was locking down hundreds of millions of people and closing manufacturing facilities. As China is the largest manufacturing country in the world, the economic repercussions were really starting to be felt. And with less manufacturing output, there were fewer container ships leaving Asia full of goods, meaning activity in ports in North America and Europe were slowing down rather quickly as well.

With fewer goods coming out of China, the international logistics systems were slowing, if not stopping. Ocean freighters were not sailing because of the lack of goods available for shipment. Docks and ports are working at a fraction of their capacity for both exporting and importing facilities. Shortly thereafter, the tsunami of infections overtook Europe. Italy locked down their country. Iran and Spain were highly infected. And the U.S. finally had to accept the reality that the virus was here to stay and invade unless serious action was taken.

Borders were closed, air travel curtailed if not suspended outright, cruise ships were quarantined, tourism all over the planet plummeted, restaurants and theaters were closed, and entertainment and sporting events and leagues were canceled. We briefly engaged with the concept of the metaverse, albeit in a somewhat premature manner. Naturally, industries and ventures with zero to lean logistics that rely on digital delivery, streaming services, home delivery systems, and gaming experienced a surge in growth since they inherently operate within virtual supply chains.

Conversely, other industries with traditional supply chains responded by proactively mitigating potential risks and bolstering collective response capabilities. For instance, in France, LVMH Moet Hennessy, which carries brands like Dior and Givenchy shifted their production focus to manufacturing hand sanitizers instead of alcohol and perfume, showcasing their adaptability and commitment to the greater good.

Automakers pivoted to produce low-cost, simplified versions of ventilators a critical medical equipment to aid in the coronavirus response. War measure acts have been enacted, or are being considered to be enacted, to force the conversion of factories to manufacture high-priority shortage items like medical supplies. With the lowered demand for automobiles, and lockdowns in factories, many end-products have stopped being produced or at the same levels of the pandemic. This was quite visible in chip production.

However, if we closely look at one of the root causes of the semiconductor crisis, we will see a big bottleneck. Global industries have almost completely outsourced all chip production to Taiwan. It is cheaper to produce chips in Taiwan since 92% of the world's chip production comes from there. Looking retrospectively, a potentially huge disaster in Taiwan will disrupt production for the whole world, which we have witnessed with the Russian Aggression on Ukraine. The disruption caused by the conflict in Ukraine had a ripple effect on the semiconductor industry, resulting in supply chain disruptions that affected the entire world.

This scenario sheds light on the inherent risks associated with concentrating essential production processes in a single geographic location. The reliance on Taiwan for the majority of chip manufacturing highlights the potential magnitude of a potential disaster or disruption in that region, as observed during the Russian aggression on Ukraine. This serves as a reminder of the importance of diversifying supply chains and spreading production capacities across multiple regions to mitigate risks and enhance global supply chain resilience.

While chips are not essential for human survival, albeit a big accelerator of thriving, wheat and vegetable oil are more deeply linked with human survival based on the WFP estimations. For instance Ukraine supplies up to 16% of the world's corn exports and more than 40% of the world's sunflower oil. A recent BBC report in 2022 noted that Egypt and Bangladesh each get about one-quarter of their wheat from Ukraine. As the climate crisis affects the most vulnerable the most, Ukrainian grain means a lot for the world's poorest and most vulnerable as the price of wheat in Africa is up by 45%. The energy crisis, chip shortages, and food blockades resulted in too much money running after too few goods, hence these shortages triggered a spiral of inflation. But what are the lessons that we can learn and apply, as founders, to make sure we stay ahead of these challenges by pivoting how we procure things to build products and services?

A 100% Resilient Supply Chain Isn't Sustainable

The process of globalization, while bringing numerous benefits, has also introduced vulnerabilities into supply chains, making them susceptible to disruption. These vulnerabilities become glaringly apparent during times of crises, be it a financial meltdown, a global pandemic, or a political conflict. The fragilities that arise in such situations have been further exacerbated by the tendency of firms to eliminate excess capacity, such as reducing inventory levels or cutting back on reserve personnel with the necessary skills to address problems effectively. According to the 2022 J.P Morgan study, COVID has disrupted supply chains in two major ways: surging demand for imported consumer goods in the West due to pandemic work from home trends and other home improvement spending, and a decline in workers required to maintain and operate these supply chains. As a result, supply chains have become less resilient, leaving companies exposed to unexpected shocks. Considering that the labor force participation in the median economy in Europe could decline by more than 10 percentage points by 2050 in the absence of migration, such disturbances will continue. In response to these challenges, organizations have been compelled to seek alternative modes of logistics to ensure the continuity of operations during the pandemic. Global companies have undertaken remarkable adaptations, such as repurposing their manufacturing facilities to produce essential items or reconfiguring their logistical routes to overcome disruptions caused by the crisis at hand. These strategic shifts demonstrate the necessity for agile and flexible supply chain strategies that can quickly respond and adapt to changing circumstances. We'll get more into how founders can implement these helpful changes later on.

The pursuit of these alternative logistics approaches underscores the importance of resilience in supply chains. Companies are recognizing the need to reevaluate their practices and embrace a more robust framework that includes contingency plans, diversified sourcing, and the cultivation of adaptable production capabilities. By doing so, they can better navigate future crises and minimize the adverse impacts on their operations and customers.

In brief a 100% resilient supply chain is not sustainable as it can lead to increased costs and reduced flexibility. Instead, focus on strategic partnerships with multiple suppliers to ensure continuity and reduce disruption. As the founder of a startup, consider diversifying your supply chain and establishing backup options for essential resources to maintain business stability in the face of unexpected events

Leaders Win Through Logistics

As the author of "In Search of Excellence" Tom Peters famously said, "Leaders win through logistics. Vision, sure. Strategy, yes. But when you go to war, you need to have both toilet paper and bullets at the right place at the right time. In other words, you must win through superior logistics." This statement highlights the crucial role that logistics plays in the success of any business, particularly during times of crisis. Founders who prioritize logistics and supply chain management can gain a competitive advantage by ensuring that their businesses have the necessary resources and goods available when and where they're needed. By doing so, they can improve their resilience and be better prepared for any future crises that may arise. The pandemic has shown that logistics is not just a support function, but a critical component of a business's success. Founders need to understand the importance of logistics and invest in it. This includes having a dedicated logistics team or role that is responsible for managing the supply chain, tracking inventory, and ensuring timely delivery of goods. Businesses with a robust logistics strategy are better equipped to handle disruptions in the market and gain a competitive advantage.

Reverse Logistics are Critical in Combating Crises

In addition to the logistic roles, there is a hidden value in alternative methods. Reverse logistics is a pivotal lever in the fight to combat any crisis. As an alternative method, reverse logistics refers to the process of managing the return of goods from the point of consumption to the point of origin. During the COVID-19 pandemic, reverse logistics played a crucial role in the supply chain as it allowed for the proper handling of products that were returned or not needed, ensuring that they were not wasted and could be repurposed or disposed of in an environmentally friendly manner.

One remarkable example of how reverse logistics was used during COVID-19 can be found in the management of returns and refunds for e-commerce purchases. With more people shopping online due to lockdowns and restrictions, there was a significant increase in the number of returns and refunds requested by customers. This presented a challenge for e-commerce companies that had to manage the volume of returns, handle the processing of refunds, and ensure that returned items were not wasted and could be resold or repurposed.

To address this challenge, e-commerce companies had to establish reverse logistics processes to manage the return of products. This included coordinating with logistics providers to arrange for the pickup and transport of returned items, ensuring that they were properly packaged and labeled, and establishing processes for the inspection, refurbishment, or repurposing of returned items. In some cases, companies also partnered with third-party logistics providers to manage the returns process and handle the logistics of product refurbishment and resale.

By implementing effective reverse logistics strategies, e-commerce companies were able to reduce waste, recover some of the costs associated with returns, and improve customer satisfaction by ensuring a smooth and efficient returns process.

When your supply lines are disrupted the ability to reclaim and refurbish products and component materials can serve as ways to restore some level of supply continuity. Any materials that you can yield through these activities will certainly augment your supply levels and help you buy time until the rest of your supply restoration actions kick in.

Hyperlocalisation and the Rise of DIY Culture Affect Markets

It's not a surprise that the COVID-19 pandemic has brought with it stress, fear, frustration, and anxiety. Not only are people missing their friends and family but the "normal" we all have been living in for decades has been flipped upside down.

Mental health and self-care have been important topics since the outbreak started. As we discussed in the earlier chapter the deep wave was with the local production and passion or creator economy. DIY projects and crafting can actually help to reduce stress levels, improve anxiety and mood as well as build a feeling of connection between yourself and the world around you. It's of little surprise that many people are turning to some form of creativity while waiting out the global pandemic, whether it was breadmaking, gardening, or sewing. However, this is not just a fleeting trend, it highlights a bigger emerging change. The emergence of distributed manufacturing (DM) is examined as a new form of localized production, distinct from previous manifestations of multi-domestic and indigenous production. Additive manufacturing, more commonly referred to as **3-D printing** has been changing the production process. Albeit, the change is not limited to 3-D printing itself. With the recent technological breakthrough with blockchain technologies and lowered barriers to creating content, co-founder of Variant Fund, Li Jin suggests that shared ownership and control of online platforms is the way forward. Considering the growth of distributed finance, energy grids, and ledgers, the production will be soon too distributed along with the talent.

Antifragility of a Venture is Beyond Resilience and Robustness

The pandemic has shown that being resilient and robust is not enough. As Nassim Nicholas Taleb suggests, businesses need to be antifragile, meaning they thrive in uncertainty and chaos. Founders need to build their businesses in a way that allows them to adapt quickly to changes in the market. This includes having a flexible and lean supply chain that can quickly respond to disruptions in the market. An antifragile business can turn adverse events into opportunities for growth with quick and effective pivots.

While some ventures have managed to weather the storm, others have faltered and crumbled under the immense pressure. The crisis has highlighted the importance of resilience and robustness in business operations, but there's another concept that has gained increasing attention in recent times – antifragility.

As we discussed antifragility in earlier chapters, antifragile systems not only withstand stressors but also benefit from them. In other words, they thrive in chaos and uncertainty, rather than merely surviving. In the context of startups, antifragility is a crucial concept that goes beyond just resilience and robustness. COVID-19 was a clear indicator for businesses to move beyond the just-in-time inventory system, popularized by Toyota in 70s-80s Japan. The pandemic has exposed the fragility of global supply chains and the risks associated with relying too heavily on a single supplier or region. The scarcity of N95 masks and other medical supplies early in the pandemic was a clear example of this vulnerability.

As a startup founder, the pandemic has highlighted the importance of moving beyond just being resilient and robust. It's practical to strive for an antifragile venture, which means actively seeking growth opportunities during challenging times, embracing change, diversifying revenue sources, and creating adaptable systems that can benefit from disruptions instead of merely withstanding them.

That is why ventures need to adopt a more agile approach to building new supply chains including software companies. Notion that There is no "software supply chain" is totally wrong as we have witnessed this with the bottlenecks of chip production. This could involve diversifying suppliers and regions, investing in local production facilities, and leveraging emerging technologies such as blockchain, 3-D printing, and generative AI to improve supply chain transparency and resilience.

Moreover, ventures should also focus on building a culture of antifragility within their organizations. This means encouraging experimentation, embracing failure as a learning opportunity, and fostering a mindset of continuous improvement. In an antifragile venture, both founders and employees are encouraged to challenge assumptions and take calculated risks to drive innovation and growth for a long time to come.

CHAPTER 11: BACK TO THE NATURE

Two roads diverged in a wood, and I—
I took the one less traveled by,
And that has made all the difference.
                    Robert Frost

As economies slowed down and strict lockdown measures were enforced, industries and human activities came to a halt, resulting in a significant decrease in harmful emissions such as NO_2 and CO_2. The previously polluted skies gradually cleared, unveiling a refreshing purity in the air and cleaner water sources. The world observed the positive impact of reduced human influence, as nature appeared to breathe a sigh of relief, embracing the chance to heal and regenerate. The COVID-19 pandemic has forced us to reevaluate our lives and the way we interact with the world around us. One of the lessons we can take away from this experience is the importance of reconnecting with nature and practicing self-cultivation. In this chapter, we will explore the benefits of returning to nature, the difference between vegetative and generative growth, and what these concepts mean when it comes to building for the planet.

The Benefits of Nature

During the pandemic, many people found refuge in nature. With restrictions on travel and social gatherings, outdoor activities such as hiking, gardening, and bird-watching became increasingly popular. Studies have shown that spending time in nature can have a positive impact on our mental and physical health. Time spent in green spaces has been linked to reduced stress, improved mood, and increased creativity. Nature also provides us with a sense of perspective and helps us to appreciate the beauty of the world around us.

One of the lessons we can take from the pandemic is the importance of prioritizing our relationship with the natural world. Why? Because anything that isn't rooted in truth within nature has begun to break and crumble. By spending more time outside and engaging in activities that connect us with the environment, we can improve our well-being and become more mindful of our impact on the planet. Founders should consider taking a step back and prioritize moments of calmness in nature. Retreats prove to be beneficial investments for founders, as they provide the opportunity to temporarily relinquish control and let someone else or even nature take the lead, leading to rejuvenation and renewed focus on their entrepreneurial journey.

Vegetative Growth vs. Generative Growth

As a development economist by training, I have witnessed how the modern economies are obsessed with the notion of growth. Leaders and politicians measure economic prosperity through Gross Domestic Product (GDP), track stock market performance, and strive for continuous personal and professional advancement. However, by looking to nature one can see that growth can take many forms, and it's essential to consider what type of growth is truly beneficial. In biology, we see this distinction in the concepts of vegetative and generative growth. Vegetative growth refers to the development of leaves, stems, and roots, which are crucial for a plant's survival. On the other hand, generative growth leads to the creation of flowers, fruits, and seeds, which play a vital role in the plant's reproductive cycle.

When I think about building for the planet, I am referring to the generative (not exclusively regenerative) practice of innovating and creating seeds of change. This approach is about more than just sustaining what we already have; it's about creating something new and impactful that will last beyond our lifetimes. Just as a tree cannot grow indefinitely, we must recognize that our venture has a purpose and that we need to create a legacy of positive change for future generations. Building for the planet is about investing in sustainable and regenerative solutions that will create a better world for all of us. It's about recognizing that generative growth is the key to creating a healthier, more equitable, and more sustainable future.

The same is true for companies as we are often equipped with the mindset of infinite growth. In the age of multi-trillion dollar companies, the start-up ecosystem is in the constant pursuit of chasing unicorns. However, unicorns do not exist in nature. As during the last 150 years we have distanced ourselves from nature, it is not so surprising to see this is a modern trend. However, prior to the industrial age, the economies were in a constant cycle of circularity. The key is to make our economies circular again, as nature intended.

By observing natural cycles and embracing circular economy principles, we can reestablish the balance that has been disrupted. This entails minimizing waste, extending product lifecycles through repair, reuse, and recycling, and fostering regenerative practices that mimic the resilience and efficiency found in natural systems. Such an approach requires a shift in mindset, where the focus shifts from linear growth to a holistic perspective that considers the long-term well-being of both businesses and the planet.

By making our economies circular once again, we can strive for harmony with nature and create a sustainable future that respects the finite resources of our planet. It is through this alignment that we can achieve prosperity while honoring the principles of circularity that have shaped our world for centuries.

There are No Passengers on Spaceship Earth; We Are All Crew

The words *economy* and *ecosystem* have the same etymological root, eco. One refers to household management while the latter means the knowledge of a household. However, the COVID-19 pandemic has highlighted that the foundation of our modern economy is built at the expense of our ecosystem. This duality showed the importance of healthy ecosystems for sustaining healthy economies. To maximize the pandemic as a pivot point for ecosystem conservation and purposeful action, we need to take a holistic approach that recognizes the interconnectedness of ecological and economic systems. Nature article dives deeper into ecosystem-economy relations and how we can get past the challenges posed by the COVID-19 pandemic to biological conservation. Let's get into some of the main lessons below:

- Improve empirical support to develop conservation strategies: To effectively conserve ecosystems, we need to have a good understanding of their ecological dynamics, as well as the socioeconomic and cultural factors that influence them. By investing in research that generates empirical support, we can develop evidence-based conservation strategies that are more likely to succeed in achieving ecological and economic sustainability.

- Manage threats using integrated and comprehensive approaches: The threats to ecosystems are complex and multifaceted and require integrated and comprehensive approaches to manage them effectively. By bringing together different stakeholders, including local communities, governments, and private sector actors, we can develop solutions that are more effective, equitable, and sustainable.

- Build multi-sectoral approaches: Ecosystems are affected by multiple sectors, including agriculture, forestry, mining, and infrastructure development. By building multi-sectoral approaches that bring together different stakeholders, we can develop solutions that are more effective, equitable, and sustainable.

- Work directly with local experts and indigenous systems: Local communities and indigenous peoples have valuable knowledge and expertise about the ecosystems they inhabit. By working directly with them and incorporating their knowledge and practices, we can develop more effective and culturally appropriate conservation strategies.

- Diversify local economies: Ecosystems provide a wide range of ecosystem services that are critical for supporting human well-being, including food, water, and clean air. By diversifying local economies to include activities that are compatible with ecosystem conservation, we can create sustainable livelihoods that are less dependent on ecosystem degradation.

- Develop nature-based solutions: Nature-based solutions, such as ecological restoration, green infrastructure, and sustainable land management, can provide multiple benefits, including biodiversity conservation, climate change mitigation and adaptation, and the provision of ecosystem services. By investing in these solutions, we can achieve both ecological and economic sustainability.

- Link ecosystem approaches and circular economies: Ecosystem approaches and circular economies share common principles, including the importance of resource efficiency, waste reduction, and recycling. By linking these approaches, we can create a more sustainable and circular economy that is better aligned with ecosystem conservation and human well-being.

Having time to observe nature can help us to differentiate vegetative growth from generative growth. Generative growth is needed to sustain life on the planet and the growth of life. As one of the stakeholders of our planetary system, our role is to create harmony without being destructive. One of my favorite systems thinkers, Buckminster Fuller, coined the phrase "Spaceship Earth" to describe our planet. In his 1983 book, *Grunch of Giants*, Buckminster Fuller wrote, "I do know that technologically humanity now has the opportunity, for the first time in its history, to operate our planet in such a manner as to support and accommodate all humanity at a substantially more advanced standard of living than any humans have ever experienced." Bucky hoped that someday the resources of the planet would be equitably divided, and people all around the world would achieve a high standard of living with access to technologically-advanced housing and transportation. Once we see the planet not as a resource but as a stakeholder, we can build not only for our clients and customers but also for the planet that will host infinite generations. As the author of the Regeneration book Paul Hawken says we can end the climate crisis in one generation. In fact, our generation is the generation that uses its products and services as leverage to take care of our planet.

It is true that there are many reasons to be pessimistic as in the age of artificial intelligence and singularity, our collective intelligence has not caught up with regenerative intelligence. It also doesn't have to be all caught up. We need to appreciate the complexity of our own intelligence, which is multi-layered. Rather than being regenerative, our intelligence can generate not just language models but operating models that can restore, nurture and multiply ecosystems. We have to slow down innovation, mindless production, and meaningless growth. We should be focusing on mindful generative growth. Mindful generative growth entails a deliberate and conscious approach to progress, one that takes into consideration the long-term well-being of both our societies and the environment. It requires us to slow down, reflect on the consequences of our actions, and align our endeavors with the principles of sustainability and regeneration.

By prioritizing mindful generative growth, we can forge a path that allows for meaningful progress while respecting the limitations and interconnectedness of our world. This approach encourages the development of operating models that not only drive economic prosperity but also contribute to the restoration and nurturing of ecosystems. Through thoughtful innovation, responsible production practices, and purposeful growth, we can ensure that our collective intelligence is channeled toward building a future that is both sustainable and beneficial for all life on Earth. It is the pivotal time to build for planet.

CHAPTER 12: NAVIGATING THE NEXT WAVE

The COVID-19 pandemic has taught us many lessons that we can apply to future crises such as war, climate change, and mass migration. Here are some additional lessons that we can learn to navigate the next wave:

Discovering the Next Buddha in a Sangha

Buddha, dharma, and sangha are three precious jewels in Buddhism. Today, the presence of sangha is primarily centered around retreats, residential communities (both monastic and lay), and regular gatherings in cities. Interestingly, by envisioning the future of Buddhism, we can envision our own futures after the pandemic.

Amidst the pandemic, an upsurge in community-based platforms and approaches has unfolded, effectively utilized by tech giants such as Meta, Google, and Twitter. Suddenly, these platforms have integrated features to foster community connectivity. This marked shift towards community-focused businesses represents a departure from the past, where only a handful of social enterprises recognized the potential of collective intelligence through stakeholder mapping, identifying users and beneficiaries. However, the concept of belonging to an organization or community was not widely sought after.

In light of these developments, discovering the next Buddha in a Sangha takes on profound relevance. It symbolizes the exploration of new avenues where communities and collective intelligence play a pivotal role in shaping the future and finding innovative solutions. As we delve deeper into the transformative economics of practice, it becomes clear that the power of the sangha extends beyond traditional boundaries, opening up exciting possibilities for the emergence of enlightened beings who will guide us toward a brighter future.

Before the emergence of the community-based approach, there was a prevalent notion that entrepreneurs were the heroes and central figures within their teams. The focus was often on the visionary founder who drove innovation and steered the direction of their respective enterprises. This perspective paralleled the traditional understanding of the term *Buddha* as an enlightened being, but it went beyond its religious connotations. In society, entrepreneurs such as Elon Musk or Steve Jobs were seen as embodying the qualities of a Buddha, bringing forth transformative ideas and leading their companies to success.

However, with the rise of community-based platforms and approaches, the dynamics have shifted. The role of the founder is no longer limited to being the sole leader or hero but has evolved into that of a facilitator and catalyst for community development. The concept of the next Buddha in a sangha suggests that the potential for enlightened leadership and collective intelligence can extend beyond the individual founder to encompass the entire community.

In this new paradigm, founders have the opportunity to lead communities by nurturing an environment where collective wisdom and collaboration can thrive. They create spaces for individuals to come together, contribute their unique perspectives, and collectively shape the future of their endeavors. Instead of relying solely on the vision of a single enlightened individual, the community becomes a wellspring of diverse insights and ideas, with the founder serving as a guide, mentor, and coordinator.

The shift from the founder-centric model to a community-centric one is not a diminishing of the founder's role but rather an expansion of their influence and impact. By embracing the power of community, founders can tap into the collective intelligence, creativity, and passion of their members. They can foster a sense of ownership, belonging, and shared purpose, leading to greater innovation, resilience, and sustainable growth.

In a rapidly changing world, building a successful business is not solely about individual achievements or financial gains. It is about recognizing the inherent strength and wisdom that emerges from a collective effort—a Sangha or community. Just as the historical Buddha relied on his community of disciples, founders can harness the power of collective action, shared values, and purposeful works. This was even more evident when COVID put virtual borders between loved ones due to social distancing and fear in society.

In an era marked by globalization and digital connectivity, communities play a pivotal role in fostering a sense of belonging, support, and collective progress. Amidst this backdrop, community-based business models have emerged as a powerful force, reshaping the way we view entrepreneurship and economic development. These models prioritize collaboration, inclusivity, and social impact, nurturing not only thriving businesses but also stronger, more resilient communities. In this piece, we will explore the essence of community-based business models and delve into the benefits they bring to both local economies and the individuals they serve.

On Deck and Nothing Phone are two examples of companies that leverage community as a fundamental aspect of their business models. As a fellow of On Deck, I've witnessed their community-backed business model where communities of professionals in specific fields foster collaboration and knowledge sharing. Through fellowship programs and community events, On Deck creates a strong sense of community among its members, promoting collaboration and shared growth. Another company whose community approach I appreciate is Nothing Phone. As a tech company, Nothing actively seeks input and feedback from its community of users. They listen to their needs, preferences, and suggestions, incorporating them into product development and decision-making. This collaborative approach ensures that the final product aligns with the desires and expectations of the community. Learnings are not coming from an enlightened individual but a group of people connected to one another, connected to a leader, and connected to an idea, as Seth Godin frames: People like us do things like this.

Going Beyond AI to Utilize Multiple Intelligences

The *AI* industry saw strong hiring growth in 2020, despite the economic slowdown in other sectors due to the pandemic. This is because, in the wake of the COVID-19 outbreak, AI played a pivotal role in keeping organizations moving safely, accurately, and with minimal delays. Also, the mass adaptation of digital technologies, increased remote work and decreased in-person interactions pushed many companies to explore automation power by artificial intelligence. As the pandemic eased we have witnessed another boom around the generative AI modules. Many founders embraced artificial intelligence. As of 2021, investors poured $4.8 billion across *262* generative AI deals globally, per new data from Pitchbook.

However, artificial intelligence is not a new concept and is also not the only external intelligence that can a founder can use. Apart from AI, there are other intelligences to be utilized, and focusing only on one part can leave founders missing out on their full potential.

In addition to traditional forms of intelligence, there are other types of intelligences that we can tap into to address the challenges of our time. One such intelligence is Collective Intelligence, which emphasizes the power of collaboration and actively listening to stakeholders and people. By harnessing the diverse perspectives and knowledge of a collective, we can generate innovative solutions and make informed decisions that benefit society as a whole.

Another type of intelligence is Aesthetic Intelligence, which is initially coined by Pauline Brown. In my view, by embracing design thinking and planet-centered design, Aesthetic Intelligence can recognize the importance of design and aesthetics in creating sustainable and planet-friendly solutions. Drawing inspiration from movements like Bauhaus, we can integrate principles of functionality, beauty, and environmental consciousness to build for planet and create harmonious experiences. A concrete example of embracing Aesthetic Intelligence and applying design thinking and planet-centered design principles can be seen in the development of eco-friendly architectural solutions. Imagine a community-based organization focused on sustainable urban development. Instead of relying solely on the expertise and vision of a single founder, the organization adopts a community-centric approach, inviting architects, urban planners, environmentalists, and community members to collaborate in shaping the future of their urban spaces. In this scenario, the founder acts as a facilitator, bringing together diverse stakeholders and fostering an environment that encourages collective intelligence. Drawing inspiration from movements like Bauhaus, the community integrates principles of functionality, beauty, and environmental consciousness into their design process. Using design thinking methodologies, the community explores innovative solutions that not only address the practical needs of urban living but also prioritize sustainability and aesthetic appeal. Aesthetic Intelligence comes into play as the community recognizes the importance of design and aesthetics in creating spaces that are not only visually pleasing but also promote well-being, harmony with nature, and sustainable practices.

Lastly, another type of intelligence founders can embrace is Nature's Intelligence. NI reminds us of the wisdom embedded in the natural world. By observing and mimicking low-tech, nature-based solutions, and embracing a systemic view of life, we can develop products and services that are in harmony with the environment, promoting sustainability and resilience. These multiple intelligences combined with our own intelligence and AI can offer valuable insights and approaches that can contribute to a more holistic and inclusive approach to problem-solving and decision-making.

Cultivating Generational Mindset

The pandemic was a tough period for sure, and so will the climate crisis and world wars. However, despite such challenges, there are a few types of companies that survive for centuries. In Japan, such countries are classified as shinise. Building companies that can last for generations has innate sustainability and regeneration within their business models. In addition to the Japanese concept of *shinise* (老舗), Martin Reeves scientifically explores the longevity of companies, drawing inspiration from both biological principles and existing research such as Collins and Porras' book, 'Built to Last.'

Reeves discovered that the average company lasts only 30 years, with a 32% chance of collapse within five years. By examining long-lasting companies, he identified six principles of complex systems that contribute to their success. The first principle, redundancy, emphasizes the importance of having backups and safeguards in critical areas of operation. Diversity, the second principle, encourages the inclusion of individuals who challenge the corporate culture and bring fresh perspectives. The third principle, modularity, suggests breaking down systems into manageable parts with clear inputs, outputs, and adaptable internal designs. Adaptability, the fourth principle, stresses the need for multi-skilled employees and a willingness to change in response to evolving circumstances. Prudence, the fifth principle, advocates for responsible financial management, avoiding excessive debt and unnecessary expenses. Finally, embeddedness highlights the significance of closely integrating various components within the system while maintaining modularity.

As we discussed in the previous chapter, while infinite growth is the most sought-after concept of the 20th century, we need generative growth while adopting a generational mindset. To apply these principles, a holistic understanding of the company as a system is crucial, and long-term thinking is required, even if short-term sacrifices are necessary for sustained survival. These principles can also be applied to a one-person venture to million dollar business while, promoting regeneration, and fostering adaptability and prudence in the face of uncertainty. My question to you then is: What do you need to pivot in your business to go from a maximum of 30 years to 100 years?

Thinking with Systems

When first delving into systems thinking, grasping the concept of feedback loops proved challenging. This difficulty stemmed from the traditional approach of siloed scientific methods ingrained in our education systems. However, it is naïve to believe that things operate independently within their own isolated bubbles. In reality, myriad elements interact and intertwine. Adopting a systems thinking mindset entails both deconstructing a larger system into its constituent modules and reconstructing it as a cohesive whole. The real world presents us with constraints that can either make or break potential outcomes. Embracing the beauty and creativity of these constraints can lead to remarkable results. Take Mick Jagger's signature stage moves, for instance. They emerged from the confined space of the Rolling Stones' earliest performances, where limited room remained once the band's equipment was set up onstage. Jagger developed what he could within those constraints, and the rest is swaggering history. To explore more stories like these, "A Beautiful Constraint" is an excellent book that teaches how to transform constraints into a driving force for creativity. However, constraints represent just one aspect of a system. Embracing systemic thinking necessitates mapping the feedback loops, the circular pathways through which information or resources flow within a system. These loops can be either positive (reinforcing) or negative (balancing), and they profoundly influence the behavior and stability of the system.

Jon Brewton explains how to embrace systems thinking in 6 steps. These are Applying Systems Thinking: A Step-by-Step Process.

Define the problem or issue: Clearly articulate the problem or issue you want to address and determine the scope and boundaries of the system you will be analyzing.

Identify the components and their relationships: Map out the key components of the system and examine how they interact with each other. Consider how the components influence and are influenced by their environment.

Analyze feedback loops and emergent properties: Identify positive and negative feedback loops within the system and examine how they contribute to its behavior. Look for emergent properties that arise from the interactions between components.

Identify leverage points: Locate points within the system where small changes could lead to significant impacts on the system's behavior or outcome. This will help you prioritize interventions or solutions.

Develop interventions or solutions: Based on your analysis, propose interventions or solutions that address the root causes of the problem, rather than just the symptoms. Consider both short-term and long-term consequences, as well as potential unintended consequences.

Monitor and evaluate: Implement your proposed interventions or solutions, and monitor the system to evaluate their effectiveness. Adjust your approach as necessary to achieve the desired outcomes.

As a developer focused on startup ecosystems, I have often encountered inquiries regarding the process of mapping a system. Through numerous conversations, I have come to believe that thinking in systems necessitates a new level of cognitive engagement, often referred to as second-level thinking. This concept is eloquently introduced by Howard Marks in his book "The Most Important Thing." While first-level thinking is characterized by its simplicity and speed (remembering that speed does not equate to direction), second-order thinking delves into the depths of complexity, demanding a deliberate and thoughtful approach. By posing "And then what?" questions, we can gain insight into the potential outcomes of our products and decisions. This line of inquiry also aids in identifying the feedback loops within the system in which you or your startup operates which is essential part of the system we operate.

Creating Distributed Systems

During the pandemic, many new technologies started to gain traction and attract critical mass, such as AI, distributed ledgers, and Web 3.0. However, when we apply second-order thinking to consider what is emerging, for example, by asking the "and then what?" question, we realize that there is a lack of application in many fields. This might not be the case for AI, but these technologies can still have a significant positive impact on solving the biggest problems we will face in the coming years. As William Gibson cleverly articulated, the future is already here – it's just not evenly distributed. This also holds true for the climate crisis, as many countries are disproportionately experiencing the disadvantages of climate change compared to their actual environmental impact. This further exemplifies the significance of second-order thinking, as it prompts us to consider the interconnectedness of global systems and the potential feedback loops that contribute to the disproportionate effects of the climate crisis on certain countries, irrespective of their individual environmental impact.

The same applies to the spread of technology. However, the distribution problem of technology needs to be observed from a different angle, and it is closely related to energy resources. It is no secret that the cost of clean energy is becoming cheaper compared to fossil fuels. Moreover, what requires more attention is the way these energy sources are being obtained. Unlike traditional utility approaches, renewable energy can be cultivated off-grid with distributed infrastructures. Reflecting on how we generate energy, as Barry Lord identified in his book, the energy source we use has a direct implication for the culture we produce. For instance, with the rise of oil, paintings using oil dominated the art market. The same goes for petroleum. Since the 1950s, with the overproduction of petroleum-based products, more and more items, including content consumption, became disposable. Consequently, we have the issue of garbage islands in the middle of our oceans. However, since the 2020s, the rapid adoption of distributed, off-grid, clean energy production might indicate a distributed and regenerative mode of production for the future. Therefore, the question for founders is: In order to be future-fit, which parts of your service or product can be distributed?

Building for Planet

During the initial stages of the pandemic, the significance of flattening the curve was widely discussed. Taking prompt actions and establishing effective detection systems were vital in mitigating the adverse impacts of such a crisis. Similarly, in the context of the climate crisis, the prevailing sentiment can often be dominated by pessimism and a deluge of alarming news, triggering climate anxiety, much like what we experienced during the early days of the pandemic. In such circumstances, the ability to discern truth from misinformation becomes a crucial skill. Establishing science-based targets not only helps alleviate anxiety but also enables us to distinguish the signal from the noise. This becomes especially important considering that numerous corporations seek to leverage the ESG narrative for their marketing campaigns, although many of these campaigns merely serve as attempts to greenwash their organizations.

I believe that having a purposeful organization is the only way to sustain and attract talent in a sustainable way. With the move from a profit-maximizing shareholder mindset to impact maximization stakeholder capitalism, we need to change our understanding of growth. Infinite growth is not only unattainable but also not realistic. The planet has limited resources, which is why the economy is derived from the notion of economia, the Greek notion of management of household with limited resources. Ecology on the other hand is the science of our home, eco. As Buckminster Fuller cleverly articulated that "There are no passengers on Spaceship Earth, only crew." As the crew, our task is to build for planet. That is our mandate, that is our direction. And we have to remind ourselves that s*peed is* defined as having *no direction* - that is, *velocity is* made up of the *speed* plus a *direction* of motion. We need to innovate, ship, iterate, and design for this direction, at speed and scale.

In the last decade, the world has witnessed remarkable advancements in technology and an emergence of a new wave of talented individuals committed to overcoming the barriers that hinder our progress toward a sustainable future. This influx of young minds, explicitly dedicated to reducing greenhouse gas emissions and developing innovative solutions to preserve our planet, has ushered in a new era for climate tech.

While much of the conversation surrounding climate tech focuses on carbon removal, it is essential to acknowledge the equally critical need for action in areas such as biodiversity protection and adaptation solutions. Our planet's challenges are multifaceted, demanding a comprehensive approach that encompasses all aspects of the environment.

Climate tech stands as the paramount industry of our times, as it addresses the pressing issues that assail our planet. However, navigating this complex landscape is no easy feat. The combination of deep climate science knowledge, regulatory intricacies, funding obstacles, and technical complexities presents significant challenges to those seeking to make a difference.

Nevertheless, this year marks a turning point for climate tech. The devastating consequences of extreme weather events, including record-breaking hurricanes, uncontrollable wildfires, and rising sea levels, have ignited a sense of urgency among investors, entrepreneurs, and governments worldwide. These stakeholders have recognized the transformative potential of technology and innovation in combating climate change.

One key aspect that needs attention is the collaboration and integration between entrepreneurial talent and climate scientists and researchers. Despite their shared purpose, these two groups have often operated in separate spheres. For our collective efforts to succeed, entrepreneurs must tap into the vast knowledge and expertise of climate scientists and researchers. By fostering collaboration and facilitating cross-disciplinary dialogue, we can harness the collective power of diverse perspectives and accelerate the development of impactful solutions.

In the intricate and emotionally taxing space of climate tech, unity, and collaboration are especially crucial. Building purposeful organizations requires the collective determination of individuals who are driven by a shared vision to regenerate the Earth and protect its precious resources. Together, we can drive meaningful change and tackle the most significant challenges of our time.

The growth of climate tech investment provides a glimmer of hope. According to a PWC report on the State of Climate Tech in 2020, venture capital investment in this sector surged from $418 million in 2013 to an impressive $16.3 billion in 2019. This exponential increase represents a forty-fold growth over a span of six years. To put it into perspective, climate tech outpaced the growth rate of VC investment in AI threefold and surpassed the general VC growth rate by fivefold during the same period.

While these numbers are encouraging, they reveal that there is still ample room for expansion. In 2019, only 6% of total capital invested went into climate tech, indicating tremendous untapped potential. However, the remarkable growth rate of the sector attracts a different magnitude and quality of investors, bringing renewed optimism to the field.

Nevertheless, climate tech investments require patient capital. Achieving meaningful impact necessitates extending investment horizons, allowing for the maturation of these ventures and enabling the full realization of their potential. Venture capitalists need to recognize the long-term nature of climate tech and support the entrepreneurs and innovators who are dedicated to making lasting changes.

By aligning capital and talent, we have the tremendous opportunity to amplify our impact and create meaningful change. Purposeful organizations, united by a shared commitment to regenerate the Earth and safeguard its biodiversity, will serve as the catalysts for a sustainable future. It is the convergence of entrepreneurial energy, scientific expertise, and patient capital that holds the key to unlocking transformative solutions capable of shaping the trajectory of our planet.

Now, more than ever, we must join forces, bridging the gaps between disciplines and embracing collaboration. It is through the establishment of purposeful organizations that we can fully harness the power of talent and capital to drive positive change. This requires a collective effort, as we recognize that our actions today will reverberate into the world of tomorrow.

With an unwavering dedication to building for the planet, we can envision a future where humanity and nature coexist in harmony. Together, we have the ability to shape a world where sustainability is not just a concept, but a way of life. Let us seize this moment, unleashing our collective potential to create a future that thrives on the principles of regeneration, resilience, and shared prosperity.

CONCLUSION

Writing a book as a first-time author is a big challenge. But this is a book that I have longed to read, and throughout the writing process, I have not come across a similar work being published. While some people may argue that the pandemic is long gone, I firmly believe we still need to reflect on the past and avoid returning to the normalcy that led to the *polycrisis*.

I strongly believe that the pandemic presented us with valuable opportunities to learn, and I sincerely hope that the insights, lessons and stories I have shared here will be helpful for you in building and pivoting for the planet. Throughout the process of writing this book, I have found joy in the act of writing itself, and my greatest wish is that it will offer you both a moment of reflection and an enjoyable read.

www.ingramcontent.com/pod-product-compliance
Lightning Source LLC
Chambersburg PA
CBHW070538220526
45467CB00003B/983